This book is packed with meticulously researched verse-by-verse Biblical exposition and will be more than useful to people anywhere who are interested in the message of 'Philippians' whether in Bible Study groups or as individuals. It contains helpful questions for discussion as well as outlines for speakers.

The book also carries something very special: through its pages there runs the river of the experiences of the man who wrote *Comfy Glasgow*. The river sparkles and winks in the sunlight of his own cheerful personality. Here is Dr. Mitchell the steelworker, the schoolteacher, the academic lecturer, the poet, the family man, the evangelist and the courageous pastor pouring his heart out about the things that are his 'raison d'etre.' I'd recommend this book to anybody. It has a huge reach.

Derick Bingham, Belfast

Which of Paul's epistles is the favourite among Christians? Possibly Romans for those in the pulpit, but almost certainly Philippians for those in the pew. For this reason it is important for commentaries on the latter to be reader-friendly, and this is certainly true of this book. George Mitchell gives many a lively illustration of Paul's thought, compelling us to face its practical implications fairly and squarely.

Geoffrey Grogan,
International Christian College, Glasgow

George Mitchell's commentary on Philippians, *Chained and Cheerful*, is scholarly and spiritual, rigorous and readable, academic and accessible, filled with hefty doses of wit and warmth. I read it on an eight hour flight across the Atlantic and arrived with the feeling of my soul having been in a good warm shower.

Charles Price
Capernwray Bible School

This commentary is wonderfully alive. Information, inspiration and application jostle for the reader's attention. George Mitchell has unlocked the teaching of Philippians in a way that will serve both as a useful tool for preachers and a useful guide to individual believers. He has done his homework and knows the issues that the letter throws up and with which the scholars grapple. But he writes as a pastor with a common touch. He deftly uses some of the rich insights of older scholars but never loses sight of his own poor upbringing and life as a steelworker in 'Comfy Glasgow'. It is a delight to read, and mirrors the joy which threads its way through Philippians.

Derek Tidball,
Principal,
London Bible College

Dr. George Mitchell is pastor of Castle Street Baptist Church in Inverness, Scotland. His autobiography, *Comfy Glasgow*, was published in 1999. He is currently engaged in research into the life of Jock Troup, a well-known Scottish evangelist.

CHAINED AND CHEERFUL

PAUL'S LETTER TO THE PHILIPPIANS

GEORGE J. MITCHELL

Christian Focus

ISBN 1 85792 666 8

Published in 2001 by
Christian Focus Publications Ltd.
Geanies House, Fearn, Ross-shire,
IV20 1TW, Scotland, Great Britain.

Cover design by Alister MacInnes

Printed and bound in Great Britain by
The Guernsey Press Co. Ltd., Guernsey, Channel Islands

Contents

Dedicated to Jean,

wife, mother, encourager and organiser.

THANK YOU, THANK YOU, THANK YOU!

I, like the apostle Paul, am under obligation to so many people, that I am almost afraid to mention them in case I miss some out. I am grateful to my wife Jean and our son Finlay and daughter Janet for constant encouragement over the years, and to our daughter-in-law Fiona and son-in-law Curtis. All the dear brothers and sisters at Castle Street Baptist Church, Inverness, have been very encouraging and helpful. Malcolm Maclean and the staff at Christian Focus have given wise counsel and practical help. My brothers in ministry in Inverness, Jack Seaton and Robert Cleland, have kindly given extended loans of commentaries on Philippians. Alistair Murray and Sheila MacDougall helped with preliminary reading. I am also grateful to all the theological 'big guns' who have commented on Philippians before me.

A WORD ABOUT THE TITLE

I realise that this is one volume in a series 'Focus on the Bible', but felt that some summary title was required for the letter to the Philippians. My initial thought was 'Chained **but** Cheerful', but influenced by texts like Romans 8:35 and 37: 'Who shall separate us from the love of Christ? Shall trouble or hardship or persecution or famine or nakedness or danger or sword?...No, **in all these things** we are more than conquerors through Him who loved us', I have changed my view. It is more accurate to give the book the title 'Chained **and** Cheerful', because the point in this prison letter is not that Paul has the joy of the Lord **despite** his circumstances, but rather **in** his circumstances. This must be an encouragement to all Christians who are having a hard time! I know that this letter of the apostle Paul has been a constant source of encouragement and inspiration to me in my hard times. I am the kind of person who looks at the number of pages in a book in relation to the price before buying it. In the light of that, in order to attempt to give the maximum value for money spent on this book, I have included questions for discussion and study at the end of each chapter, which may be helpful to groups, and a series of preaching outlines at the end of the book, which may be helpful to preachers...

CHAPTER ONE

INTRODUCTORY MATTERS

Reading the New Testament letters is like eavesdropping on a telephone conversation; we have to make deductions about what we don't hear (or in this case, read), and sometimes the conclusions we arrive at have to be tentative. In the case of Philippians, we are probably considering a letter written in the early sixties A.D., which adds historical and cultural complications to the rich mixture of our thinking.

Paul's relationships with the believers in the Philippian Church were warm and friendly, and Philippians is essentially a 'Thank-You Letter' for kind gifts received, and conveys a very positive tone, across the centuries, to the modern reader.

1. The writer – Paul

Saul was the nearest rendering in English to the Greek form 'Saoul', or 'Saulos', which attempts to transliterate his Hebrew name 'Sha'ul' ('asked', of God presumably). The most frequently used form of his name in the New Testament is 'Paulos' ('the little man'), and reflects the *cognomen* (additional name) of the Roman pattern of three names for citizens. These were the *praenomen* or forename, the *nomen gentile* or family name, and the *cognomen*. Like most of us, Paul was a composite of influences, in his case **Roman, Greek and Jewish.**

Paul claimed **Roman** citizenship (Acts 22:26) by birth (Acts 22:28), one of three ways of obtaining this privilege around this time. The other two ways of gaining citizenship were by purchase (Acts 22:28) or by grant for services rendered. Some scholars have made the interesting but unsubstantiated deduction from Paul's trade as a tent-maker (Acts 18:3) that his father may have been a supplier of tents to the Roman Army, and obtained citizenship by grant. Paul's home city of Tarsus (Acts 21:39) had passed under Roman control as a result of Pompey's conquests, and became capital of the province of Cilicia (67 B.C.), retaining its autonomy as a free city. The Roman citizenship of some Tarsian Jews may date from this settlement.

The **Greek** influences on Paul were very strong. Alexander the Great had saved Tarsus from being burned down by the retreating Persians in 333 B.C. Tarsus was a university town, and an exemplar of Alexander's policy of 'polis (='city')-planting'. This was a refined combination of brain-washing and ethnic cleansing for subject states. Alexander's father, Philip of Macedon, had engaged the services of the philosopher Aristotle to act as tutor for his son, hoping no doubt that this would help to broaden the horizons of the lad, and give him a world-view. The result was, as with Napoleon much later, Alexander's achievements in war were eclipsed by his peacetime accomplishments. Veterans and wounded soldiers from Alexander's armies were encouraged to settle down, marry the local women, and spread the taste and influence of Greek culture. Cities around the Mediterranean area, and as far East as the frontiers of India, were established with baths, gymnasia, libraries, a stadium, hippodrome and theatre. The culture of body and mind flourished under a Greek parasol, so to speak, with a very palatable and entertaining version of Greek philosophy woven into the people's life-style, including their theatre-going, and their discussions at the baths, after their visit to the gymnasium. Greek was the *lingua franca* of these communities, rather like English in today's world, and we know from Paul's usage of Old Testament quotations that he was familiar with the Septuagint, a Greek translation of the Old Testament produced in Egypt about 150 B.C. The New Testament was written mainly in Koine ('common') Greek, which some scholars had regarded as almost the language of angels (1 Cor. 13:1), until they discovered it was the language of the common people, a simplified form of Classical Greek. Under the Roman Empire, and the 'Pax Romana' (which cleared the Mediterranean Sea of pirates), the road systems and common language were ready in the providence of God to carry the Good News of Jesus 'in the fulness of time' (Gal. 4:4)

The Letter to the Philippians (3:4-14) contains a significant thumbnail sketch of the **Jewish** influences on Paul. The phrase 'A Hebrew of the Hebrews', in Philippians 3:5, is best understood in terms of Paul being the Hebrew-speaking son of Hebrew parents. Probably, Aramaic was his mother-tongue (see Acts 21:40; 22:2; 26:14). He would have attended the synagogue, been taught the trade of tent-making from early teenage years, and inculcated into Judaism, which is, of course, a way of life rather than an intellectual or ritual discipline. The uncertainties of being a Jew in a hostile pagan context meant that the Jews taught even their cleverest boys a practical skill so that, if necessary, they could earn a living using their hands rather than their brains. This type of approach has made the Jews versatile and adaptable down the centuries, for example, in resettlement programmes in Israel after the Second World War.

Paul's progress in Judaism was speedy, committed and ambitious (Gal. 1:14). He became one of the Pharisees, the spiritual descendants of the Hasidim, or Loyalists (derived from the word 'hesedh'= 'loyalty, steadfast love'), of the Maccabean period, a separatist group, with special interest in the Torah, or Law. To use a description which will be meaningful only to some readers, the Pharisees were a kind of Jewish Christian Endeavour movement. As an outstanding young scholar, Paul was sent to Jerusalem to study under Rabbi Gamaliel (Acts 22:3).

Although he never met Jesus, Paul regarded him as a threat to Rabbinic Judaism, and systematically hounded the followers of the (Jesus) Way (Acts 9:1-2). Converted through a vision of the risen Christ on the road to Damascus on a persecuting mission, Paul accepted God's call to be missionary to the Gentiles. His thinking went into the melting-pot during a period of retreat in Arabia and Damascus, and he found God's direction in mission alongside his friend Barnabas in the church at Antioch (Acts 13:1ff.). His three missionary journeys, and careful missionary strategy, took him to key cities in Asia Minor and Greece, which would serve as nucleating centres for Gospel outreach. The contact with Philippi, the Philippian Church, and the Letter to the Philippians, arose out of Paul's second missionary journey.

2. The place – Philippi

Philippi (modern Filippoi) is a hill town in the department of Kavalla, in north-eastern Greece, overlooking the coastal plain, and the bay at Neapolis (Kavalla) its port, about ten miles (16 kilometres) to the south-east. There is a museum with fine artefacts at Kavalla. At Neapolis, the great *Via Egnatia*, the military road which the Romans built to link Europe and Asia, the Adriatic with the Aegean and the Bosphorus, met the sea, after passing through Philippi. The Romans built more than 372 of these wonderful highways connecting the countries of Europe, covering more than 50,000 miles of territory. The oldest was the *Via Appia*, which ran from Rome to Capua (132 miles), later extended to Brindisi, 234 miles away.

The church at Philippi was the first European church founded by Paul. It was located in Macedonia, in North-Eastern Greece, near the coastal town of Neapolis. How did the town come to be called 'Philippi' by the time the apostle Paul was writing? The personal link is with Philip II of Macedon, father of Alexander the Great. Philip's great achievement was to end the Greeks' chronic disunity by extending Macedonian control into Thrace, and consolidate his position by conquering the Greek city-states at the Battle of Chaeronea in 338 BC. Philip had annexed Philippi in 356 and fortified it for two reasons. The first was its strategic military position, located on a hill between the rivers Strymon and Nestus, overlooking the Plain of Druma and the mountain pass between Pangeus and Haemus, near its port of Neapolis. Secondly, Philip wrested the town from the Thracians in order to purloin the wealth from its gold and silver mines. The gold mines alone yielded about a thousand talents of gold annually for Philip's coffers. The plural form Philippi (rather than Philippos or Philippus) comes from its ancient past. The town grew from the old Thracian settlement of 'Krenides', or 'springs, fountains', and Philip of Macedon gave his name to each one of them, hence the plural. In 167 B.C. Macedonia was divided into four districts by Lucius Aemilius Paullus, and Philippi was included in the first district. Some scholars think the text in Acts 16:12 should be emended from *prote* to *protes* yielding the translation 'a city of the first district of Macedonia', otherwise the translation 'leading city of the district' can be used only in a general sense.

In 42 B.C. at the Battle of Philippi, Antony and Octavian, who had been political supporters of Julius Caesar, defeated his chief assassins Brutus and Cassius (who both committed suicide during or after the battle), and settled some veteran troops at Philippi. Twelve years later, after the Battle of Actium, Octavian, who had defeated the forces of Antony and Cleopatra, settled a group of Italian colonists, who had supported Antony, at Philippi. Octavian renamed the town, as coinage struck at the period shows, as 'Col (onia) Iul (ia)

Aug (usta) Philip (pensis). From that time the town had 'Italian privilege' (*ius Italicum*), and was treated as if the territory had been transplanted from Italy. Roman clothing, language and customs were incorporated into Philippian lifestyle. Hence the civic pride evidenced in Acts 16:21, compare 16:37. They were proud of being Roman colonists in a Greek context. Their two collegiate (professionally trained) magistrates had the honorary title of 'praetors'. They were called the *duo uiri* (*duum virs* or 'two men') and had in attendance, as had the two consuls in Rome, a band of lictors. The lictors carried as their badge of office the bundles (*fasces*, hence the English word 'Fascist') of elm- or birch-rods fastened together with red straps, and enclosing an axe, the head of which was left visible. These emblems signified the magistrate's right to flog wrongdoers and execute traitors. Paul and Silas were flogged at Philippi (Acts 16:22, 23).

3. The church at Philippi

Paul and his companions had been sensitive to the promptings of the Spirit regarding their strategy, and Paul had answered an invitation in a vision from a man from Macedonia (Acts 16:6-9). Some scholars think that the good Doctor Luke was the Man of Macedonia, and possibly a native of Philippi, who joined Paul and his companions at Troas. There was a medical school in the vicinity, and the 'we' passages in Acts begin from this point (compare the 'they' of Acts 16:8 with the 'we' of Acts 16:10ff.). Arguments based on the accuracy of the technical references in relation to Philippi lose their cutting edge when we realise that Luke was generally a punctilious historian, not only in relation to Philippi. They disembarked at Neapolis after a good trip, and entered Philippi. Paul's policy of going first to the synagogue to initiate any new work could not be implemented – there couldn't have been a quorum, or *minyan*, of ten (male) heads of Jewish households (the minimum to form a synagogue) in Philippi. It is interesting that Paul's vision was of a man of Macedonia, but his initial contacts there were with ladies. When they reached Philippi, they joined a prayer-group of ladies – God-fearers and Jewesses – who kept Sabbath beside the River Gangites (Acts 16:13), like the Jewish prisoners-of-war 'by the rivers of Babylon' (Psalm 137; Ezek. 1:1-3) centuries earlier.

The first European convert was a business lady called Lydia, whose heart the Lord opened like a flower to the sunlight (Acts 16:14). Lydia was an agent for the sale of the precious purple dye extracted from the juice of the fleshy madder root, for which her home region of Thyatira was famous. Paul's practice on his travels was normally to earn his living from his skill as tentmaker, so that he could preach without charge, as an example to converts and to avoid criticism of opponents that Christian preachers had mercenary motives. Here, Lydia, a lady of some means, persuaded the group to accept her hospitality. Her family also entered into an experience of 'household salvation', evidenced in baptism (Acts 16:15).

The next focus of Paul's attention was a fortune-telling slave-girl who functioned with the help of a 'pythonic spirit', whereby she became the mouthpiece of Apollo.

Apollo had multiple and complex functions in the pantheon of Greek gods: as solar god ripening earth's fruits, as archer god who shot the god of sudden death, as healer god, and as the god of prophecy and divination who pronounced judgement through intermediary priestesses, the Sibyls. As a new-born baby, so the legend goes, Apollo, nourished by the food and drink of the gods (ambrosia and nectar) immediately fought the serpent Python in the Parnassus gorge. The slave-girl at Philippi seemed to be replicating the function of the Pythia or priestess at the Delphi cave sanctuary, who uttered broken phrases and obscure words in a trance state of prophetic delirium. She was therefore the vehicle used for ventriloquistic necromancy. As she pressed her attentions on the group, giving unsolicited testimony to their spirituality (Acts 16:16-18), Paul and Silas as recognisable Jews became the target for anti-Semitic resentment, stirred up by the girl's owners. (Luke was Gentile, and Timothy half-Gentile.) There was an ugly scene, a public beating of Paul and Silas, both Roman citizens, without trial, and an earthquake at the jail where they were in custody (Acts 16:19-26). The last converts in Philippi were the jailer and his family. The furore which developed when the magistrates heard that Paul and Silas were Roman citizens, resulted in acts of appeasement and a sharp exit for the Christian preachers (Acts 16:38-40). A Christian presence sometimes precipitates trouble.

Thus, the first members of this 'missionary-minded' Philippian church were a mixed group, with strong female influences (see Phil. 4:2, 3), keen to serve the Lord and spread the gospel.

4. Where was Paul when he wrote Philippians?

(If you find technical discussion a 'turn-off', you might like to turn to Section 5!)

Paul was in prison when he wrote Philippians (Phil. 1:7,13-14) – but where? The problems arising here stem from three basic factors: the variety of Paul's periods in prison, his failure to specifically name where he is, and the distance/time explanations of the journey references in the letter. The Book of Acts mentions four imprisonments: at Philippi (16:23), Jerusalem (21:33), Caesarea (23:35) and Rome (28:16). In addition, some scholars deduce a fifth imprisonment at Ephesus from the reference in 1 Corinthians 15:32 about 'fighting wild beasts at Ephesus'. There are seven journeys envisaged from the evidence in Philippians:

1. A journey to Philippi to give news of Paul's imprisonment.
2. A journey from Philippi by Epaphroditus to hand over a gift to Paul (4:18)
3. A journey to Philippi which told of Epaphroditus' illness (2:26)
4. A journey which conveyed Philippian anxiety regarding Epaphroditus' illness (2:26)
5. A journey to Philippi by Epaphroditus to convey Paul's letter (2:25, 28)
6. A journey to Philippi by Timothy as soon as Paul's plans were clarified (2:19-23)
7. A journey to Philippi by Paul after his release from prison (2:24).

As far as the imprisonments are concerned, Philippi is of course excluded as a possibility, and Jerusalem was merely a brief period of protective custody, which excludes it.

At first sight, Caesarea seems possible. Paul was there for about two years waiting on a legal decision from Felix (Acts 24:26, 27). The technical term 'praetorium' (the Greek text uses the noun *praetorion*) used in Philippians 1:13, and the references to 'Caesar's household' in 4:22 could relate to Caesarea, since the praetorion could be used of a detachment of Imperial troops as well as a specific location, like the guard-house in Rome, or even Herod's palace in Caesarea. Caesarea seems too 'low-key', and out of the action politically and ecclesiastically for Paul's testimony to have the impact envisaged in 1:12ff. The sense of impending martyrdom inherent in Philippians 1:20ff does not match the tone of Acts 23:35. From Caesarea, a bad verdict need not have been final, as Paul could have done what he did in Acts 25:11 – appeal for a private hearing before the Emperor. Caesarea seems unlikely.

The main obstacle to Rome as the origin of the letter is the vast distance (around 1,200 miles) between Philippi and Rome – about forty days of travel. If Epaphroditus fell ill on the journey to Paul, that would reduce the time required for the journeys. His illness could have been brief, although serious. The Roman imprisonment lasted about two years, so there was time for all the journeys undertaken to be fitted in. The same argument presented about the circumstances of Paul's confinement at Caesarea hold good for Rome, to some extent, because he seemed to be under house arrest (Acts 28:30, 31). However, there is mention of a guard and chain in Acts 28:16 and 20. Circumstances could have altered for the worse after the trial. The references to the praetorion and Caesar's household fit Rome (4:22) most naturally. Paul's exhilaration at the spread of the gospel and its high profile in unpromising surroundings fits the Roman scene best.

The contrast between Paul's future plans mentioned in Romans 15:24 and 29, which indicate a journey to Spain via Rome, and his hopes of an imminent visit to Philippi, expressed in Philippians 1:25-27 and 2:24, does not present an impossible difficulty. Paul's plans were always fluid, and under the sovereignty of the Holy Spirit's leading. His ability was matched by his availability. Some of the place names in the Pastoral Letters are unattested in any plans Paul mentioned elsewhere (2 Tim. 4:13, 20; Titus 3:12). The traditional view which held the field for nineteen centuries favoured Rome as the source of the letter, and there is indirect evidence from the Marcionite Prologue, an introduction to the Bible books accepted by the heretic Marcion (c. AD 145), which said it was sent from Rome.

Ephesus as the place of origin has been strongly championed by, among others, W. Michaelis. There is no mention or hint in Acts of an Ephesian imprisonment. It is merely an inference drawn from the Corinthian correspondence (1 Cor. 15:32). The shorter distances required for the journeys mentioned certainly suit the data better (it would take about ten days maximum to sail from Philippi to Ephesus). The inscriptional evidence in relation to Ephesus fits Philippians 1:13 and 4:22. There would be a body of troops in Ephesus (as administration centre for the province of Asia) which would fit the praetorium definition. A visit to Philippi could be fitted into Acts 20:1-6, as well as Timothy's travels.

The major difficulty in accepting the Ephesus hypothesis is that it is too easy! One of the basic criteria in textual criticism and hermeneutics is to accept the 'difficult reading'. Hence, we are stuck with Rome, with all the problems associated with that choice, and a letter written in the early sixties.

5. Authenticity and unity

There are such strong internal signs of the letter's apostolic authenticity, as Paul bares his soul here when writing to his friends, and such weighty external acceptance of the letter as Pauline, that we need not spend time on this issue.

Interpolation theories focus on the note of thanks (4:10-20) and the warning to trouble-makers (3:2ff.). The former could have been written separately to accompany

Epaphroditus, and included later (according to F. F. Bruce), and the latter is better taken as an interruption rather than an interpolation. Paul's 'finally' in 3:1 (like that of most preachers!) is not to be taken too strictly or mechanically. His writing in 3:2ff. may be a reaction to news he has just heard.

6. Themes

Although Paul was in good relationships with the Philippian believers, he was not blind to their faults. The Philippian church was not a perfect church. There were rivalries and personal ambitions which had to be addressed (2:3-4; 4:2). The believers had to be warned against the Judaisers (3:1-3). Perfectionist tendencies had to be curbed (3:12-14). Carnal appetites which undermined God's law had to be condemned (3:18-19).

The letter has as its main theme an expression of thanks for repeated generosity. It also commends Timothy and Epaphroditus to the Philippian church (2:19-29), and calls it to stand firm in the face of persecution (2:15-16).

The letter also contains a significant outline of Paul's origins and attitudes (4:4-14), which does not occur elsewhere.

Chapter 2:5-11 contains one of the finest Christological passages in the New Testament. It is interesting that Paul's response to false teaching or sub-standard Christian living is a very positive presentation of who Jesus is (compare Colossians 1:15-20). One old preacher said that the best cure for frost in the pews is a good fire in the pulpit. The story is told of the U.S. Treasury trainee who asked, after a lengthy session studying $100 bills, when they would be studying counterfeit. He was told that they did not spend time studying counterfeit, because if they knew the real thing, they would recognise counterfeit easily. In what may be an early Christian hymn, perhaps composed by Paul himself, the Philippians (and us) are shown the 'real thing' in the stages of Christ's divine status and character, his self-emptying and his exaltation by God the Father. So high a view of Christ exposes the shoddiness of any false presentation of him or his gospel.

The theme of the gospel (there are nine occurrences of the word *euangelion*) is important in the Letter, because it forms the basis of Christian *koinonia* (fellowship – three occurrences) and Christian joy (sixteen occurrences in various noun and verbal forms). This joy has nothing fake or spasmodic about it, but is the deep-seated contentment of a heart at ease with God, and expresses itself, not in a vacuous 'evangeli-grin', but a confident radiance in the most unpromising or threatening circumstances. Paul would strongly agree that the Holy Spirit's presence in our lives does not mean that we jettison our brains. On the contrary, he makes at least twelve references to cerebral processes in assessing Christian priorities (e.g. 1:10, 25; 2:2, 3; 3:7, 8, 10, 13, 19; 4:6, 7, 8). A further recurrent theme in the letter is the Christian hope of life after death (1:6, 23; 2:10, 11; 3:10-11, 20-21).

Structure and Content of the letter to the Philippians

A. HELLO AND THANKS   1:1-11

B. THE CAUSE OF CHRIST   1:12-30

    Known in Restriction   1:12-14

    Preached in Contention   1:15-20

    Embodied in Expectation   1:21-30

C. THE CONDESCENSION OF CHRIST   2:1-30

Phase One:The Call to Humility   2:1-4

    The Criterion of Humility   2:5-11

Phase Two:The Continuance of Humility   2:12-18

    Copybook Humility:

    Timothy/Epaphroditus   2:19-30

D. CONFIDENCE IN CHRIST   3:1-21

Phase One: Beware   3:1-6

Phase Two: Assess/Anticipate   3:7-21

E. CONTENTMENT IN CHRIST   4:1-20

    Sharing with Others   4:1-3

    Controlling Yourself   4:4-9

    Conquering your Circumstances   4:10-20

F. FINAL FAREWELLS   4:21-23

Summary of Philippians Chapter One

Paul and Timothy are writing this as people at Christ's disposal, to all the varied patchwork of believers (not just a keen elite) at Philippi. Their heavenly calling incorporates them into God's on-going programme of holiness, with a negative aspect of separation from sin, and a positive aspect of dedication to purity. They are 'in Christ' as their natural environment, their family atmosphere and their dominating influence. Their heavenly vocation is 'earthed' to the Roman colony of Philippi, where their practical life as Christians is under a leadership which involves spiritual oversight and loving service. This life is based on God's active kindness (grace) and Christ's positive gift (peace).

The thought of these believers stimulates Paul to prayer and joy, peace and confidence, in a God who is committed to them, and to Paul their brother, who is a prisoner. He longs for a multiplication of spiritual insight and righteous fruit in their lives so that God will have greater glory.

Paul's state as a prisoner has resulted in positive advantages for the spread of the gospel, even where the preaching is rooted in contentious or ambitious motives.

Paul hopes that he will be delivered from prison, but his real desire, living or dead, is that Christ will be exalted in his body. The apostle calls the believers to godly living, and to taking a brave stand for the gospel, especially in the face of suffering.

Summary of Philippians Chapter Two

The blessings of union with Christ – encouragement, comfort, fellowship and tender concern – should lead to a spiritual unity of purpose which results in humility. Conceit and selfishness are inappropriate in such a behaviour pattern. Such loving interest should reproduce a Christ-like attitude.

Christ Jesus had as His innate characteristic an essentially divine nature. He regarded His equality as Son with God the Father as neither to be reached out for (because it was already His) nor to be selfishly clung to as His personal prize. His real humanity is seen in the self-emptying sacrifice of divine qualities in order to assume genuinely what was essentially a servant nature. He submitted temporarily to an earthly lifestyle. The glory of His character is seen in two great voluntary acts – self-humiliation, and obedience to death (unlike the rest of us, for whom death is the necessary consequence and penalty for our human sin). The extent of His love is seen in His voluntary submission to death on a cross – a criminal's punishment to Romans, and anathema to Jews, because in their thinking the victim came under God's curse. God the Father has authenticated Christ Jesus by resurrection and ascension, and has granted Him the name LORD, to grace His exalted manhood. The great acts of Jesus mean that His human name forms the basis for universal confession (not merely acknowledgement) of His Lordship, whether under grace or under judgement. The passage which began with Christ Jesus sharing the glory of the Father, ends with human beings enhancing that glory by confession.

The outworking of salvation is a blessed partnership between God and humanity. Christians are meant to shine positively and purely in a dark and hopeless world. Living of such quality will make Paul's suffering, and even his death, so worthwhile.

Paul commends Timothy as an unselfish worker. Paul will also send back Epaphroditus as a fellow-worker and a fellow-soldier, whom God's mercy has spared from a life-threatening illness. He should be welcomed and honoured.

Summary of Philippians Chapter Three

It is good to rejoice in the Lord, and to be wide awake to those who spread false teaching, with a wrong emphasis on conformity to physical rituals like circumcision as a basis for self-confidence before God. Paul lists the advantageous features of his former life – timely circumcision into a favoured tribe of Israel, Hebrew-speaking son of Hebrew parents, eager participation in Pharasaic Torah-study, persecuting activity against Christians, living flawlessly as a law-keeper.

Paul has now repudiated all such advantages in the light of his personal knowledge of Christ, whose righteousness imputed and imparted through faith, ranked his former status and achievements as trash. Paul is now spurred on to a deeper conformity to the life-and-death pattern established by Jesus as the basis for Christian living.

Paul has far to go as a Christian. He feels gripped by Christ, and driven on by Him to fulfil the full implications of God's upward call.

The dark side of living exhibited by the enemies of the Cross should act as a powerful incentive for Paul and his fellow-believers. They should live hopefully and expectantly, as those who have staked a claim for heavenly citizenship, and look forward to the Lord Jesus Christ's returning and transforming power being exercised personally on their behalf. This will prove to be a stabilising hope for all of them.

Summary of Philippians Chapter Four

The stability Paul calls for is undermined by personal disagreements. Paul calls for helpful partnership with his fellow-warriors in the gospel. The apostle commands a continual spirit of rejoicing, coupled with gentleness. Prayer is a strong antidote for anxiety, and fosters a strong sense of God's peace as a protective presence.

The apostle encourages them to cherish and model the positive graces exhibited in his life when he was with them.

A spirit of thanksgiving for their gifts leads him into an expression of personal contentment in every circumstance, and a constant reliance on God's strength. He recalls repeated acts of kindness by the Philippian church, and this 'last fragrant offering' brought by Epaphroditus. They share mutual faith in God's abilities to meet their needs. After a cluster of final greetings, he prays for God's grace to be with their spirits.

QUESTIONS FOR DISCUSSION

1. Paul's background affected his later life. Discuss any ways in which you can trace God's hand in your background.

2. Read Acts 16:6-12. How did God guide Paul and his friends to Philippi?

3. Read Acts 16:16-18. Are people today interested in fortune-telling? Give some examples, if possible.

4. What kind of impression of Christ and His servants did Paul and his friends project in dealing with the slave-girl?

5. Read Acts 16:22-25. Discuss Bonhoeffer's statement that 'the badge of Christianity is suffering'.

6. How did the jailer show that he was converted?

7. Acts 16 reveals a mixed bunch of people finding Christ at Philippi. Discuss the richness of mixture in your church.

HELLO AND THANKS
1:1–11

[1]Paul and Timothy, servants of Christ Jesus,

To all the saints in Christ Jesus at Philippi, together with the overseers and deacons;

[2] Grace and peace to you from God our Father and the Lord Jesus Christ.

[3]I thank my God every time I remember you. [4] In all my prayers for all of you, I always pray with joy [5]because of your partnership in the gospel from the first day until now, [6]being confident of this, that he who began a good work in you will carry it on to completion until the day of Christ Jesus.

[7]It is right for me to feel this way about all of you, since I have you in my heart; for whether I am in chains or defending and confirming the gospel, all of you share in God's grace with me. [8]God can testify how I long for all of you with the affection of Christ Jesus.

[9]And this is my prayer: that your love may abound more and more in knowledge and depth of insight, [10]so that you may be able to discern what is best and may be pure and blameless until the day of Christ, [11]filled with the fruit of righteousness that comes through Jesus Christ – to the glory and praise of God.

Before we begin to look in detail at this little gem of a letter, whose 104 verses sparkle with truth, it is only fair that the reader knows the presuppositions and ground-rules which motivate the writer of this volume.

My first comment would be that I take seriously the summing-up of Scriptural prophecies in 2 Peter 1:21: 'Men they were, but, impelled by the Holy Spirit, they spoke the words of God' (New English Bible). The verb translated 'impelled' here is used in Acts 27:15 of the wind driving the ship Paul was in when it was shipwrecked. The idea therefore in 2 Peter 1 is that the people who spoke or wrote the Scriptures retained their personality and individuality, but their sails were filled, as it were, by the Holy Spirit. When we take 2 Timothy 3:16 into account, 'All Scripture is God-breathed', then we are dealing here with a divine source-book, written by human authors. The Bible therefore does not merely contain the Word of God among other writings, nor does it become the Word of God when the Holy Spirit fastens a section of it on our minds or attention, but it is intrinsically and inherently the Word of God, standing on its own feet, with its own authority. J. Packer points out a helpful parallel between the Person of Christ and the content of Scripture, claiming that we have in both cases a perfect combination of the human and the divine.

Another point I would like to make is that since I was converted to Christ/born again/saved from a non-church background, I am biassed in favour of the Bible, and am willing to suspend judgement where necessary on sections I do not yet understand, while accepting the whole of Scripture as the Word of God. James 1:18 is apposite here: 'He chose to give us birth through the word of truth...' God's treatment of us in grace pre-disposes us to trust the Bible. As we attempt seriously to grapple with what is initially long ago and far away, we discover the value of Scripture not only as we elucidate its meaning, but as we discover God is speaking to us today, at the threshold of the twenty-first century, through a first-century letter written to a first-century church. J. B. Phillips compared the experience of this kind of discovery with that of an electrician being sent to re-wire an old house, and finding that the power was still surging through its electrical systems.

HELLO. When we receive letters, we have often to look at the end to see who wrote them. This was not the case in the ancient world. The first two verses of the Letter to the Philippians follow the pattern of ancient letter-writing – giving the names of the writer and the addressees, and sharing a greeting. So Paul is not cultivating a fan club here, although his name coupled with Timothy's would be highly evocative in the minds of the readers, who would have instant recall of a kaleidoscope of events involving family and church gatherings, the townspeople and the civic authorities. They would remember the inception of their fellowship life, from the inauspicious prayer gathering at the river bank, the conversion of Lydia and the opening of her heart and home to the gospel, through the very public exposure of gospel power in the healing of the demented slave-girl, the humiliation of public beating and imprisonment for God's servants, the earthquake and the conversion of the jailer, and all the tortuous steps of faith which had followed.

Paul was a 'team player', and young Timothy was a vital team member. He was young, for in 1 Timothy 4:12 he is told, 'Don't let anyone look down on you because you are young.' Paul refers to him as his 'son' in 1 Timothy 1:2 and 2 Timothy 1:2 and 2:1. We are probably given a clue about Timothy's nature in 2 Timothy 1:7 and 8: 'for God did not give us a spirit of timidity'... and in 2 Timothy 2:1: 'You then, my son, be strong in the grace that is in Christ Jesus', which probably indicates that Timothy was a shy lad. The instruction about the medicinal use of wine 'because of your stomach and frequent illnesses' in 1 Timothy 5:23 indicates that he was physically fragile.

Timothy was a man on the way to becoming the kind of man God can use. The essential elements in the making of a man of God are set out in 2 Timothy chapter 1 – parental background (1:5), spiritual gift (1:6), Christian friendship (1:2, 4) and divine grace (1:9-10) – a composite mixture of qualities useful to God in missionary service. The key criterion for usefulness on God's team is of course *availability* rather than ability.

Paul does not have to 'swing his stripes' as an apostle, because his apostolic status is not under question or attack from the Philippian Christians in the same way as it was from the Corinthian Christians (compare 1 Corinthians 1:1). Paul and Timothy are **'servants'** ('*douloi*'), 1:1. Despite the negative vibes this name would conjure up, it is good for a preacher to be known as a 'servant of Christ Jesus'. In the Graeco-Roman world of the first century, the word evokes images of utter slavery, of servants who broke a wine-glass being fed to piranha fish, and so on. Even where the bond-slave had a relatively easy life-style, as children's attendant, for example, he was never more than a chattel, listed on a farmer's inventory as a 'speaking tool' to distinguish him from animals, which were classified as 'dumb tools'. There were vast numbers of slaves in the Roman Empire, so many that the Senate decided after debate not to issue uniforms for slaves in case this would inspire rebellion.

The Old Testament concept of the servant (Hebrew, '*ebhedh*), carried with it, by way of contrast, the idea of nobility and dignity, which expands our understanding of New Testament usage. Moses is called 'my servant' (Exod.

35

14:31; Num. 12:7), and so are the prophets, as people who are intimately aware of His revelation (Amos 3:7; Mic. 3:8). The formula in the Old Testament translated 'oracle of Yahweh' (ne'um Yahweh) occurs around 400 times. The Hebrew term *ne'um* is probably an onomatopoeic word, 'a murmur, a whisper of Yahweh', a word of the intimate murmurings of important issues around the camp-fire, late at night. God's servants the prophets are 'in the know'.

After surveying the use of the term 'servant' in Scripture, two eminent scholars (Walter Zimmerli and Joachim Jeremias) give a comprehensive definition of a 'servant' as 'someone who is at the disposal of someone else'. Even although we are ordinary people of God, and knew that already, it is good to have it confirmed by academic 'heavyweights'! In our working lives, sometimes our understanding of the servant concept has been deepened when we find ourselves in situations where we seemed trapped by our circumstances, and unable to escape being at the total disposal of our bosses. My sympathies for people in the hotel trade were broadened after a short spell as a hotel dishwasher during a summer vacation, trapped in a room provided by the management, and called on, so it seemed, whenever it suited their whim. I remember later, when I was teaching history to Glasgow children, painting with a heavy brush the harsh lot of a serf in the Middle Ages, when a pupil, carried away with the enormity of the injustice of it all, blurted out that he wouldn't obey his master. When I asked him how he would defend himself in that situation of slavery, he said he would call in his mother!

As the references develop here, the *earthly location* of being at God's disposal as His **servants ...at Philippi** (1:1) is matched by their *heavenly vocation* as **saints in Christ Jesus** (1:1). The gathered fellowship of believers in any local church is a corporate expression of God's dynamic plan for the developing holiness of His people. 1 Peter 1:15, 16 helps to clarify this: 'But just as He who called you is holy, so be holy in all you do; for it is written "Be holy, because I am holy."' The highest claim any believer can make is that he is 'one of the saints', because the expression is always a corporate one in the New Testament. There are no references to an individual saint.

The saints are **in Christ** in different senses:

(1) They are 'in Christ' as their *natural environment*. Like the tadpole becoming a frog, with land rather than water as its natural environment, or like the caterpillar being transformed into a butterfly, believers are metamorphosed into new life in Christ. Second Corinthians 3:18 uses the imagery of a veil and a mirror: 'And we, who with unveiled faces all reflect the Lord's glory, are being transformed into His likeness with ever-increasing glory, which comes from the Lord, who is the Spirit.' In 2 Corinthians 5:17 the apostle sums up Christian experience: 'Therefore, if anyone is in Christ, he is a new creation; the old has gone, the new has come!'

(2) Believers are also 'in Christ' as their *family atmosphere*. They are no longer the victims of the poisonous and corrosive influences which shaped their behaviour in the past. United by the love-ties of the precious blood of Christ shed for them (1 Pet. 1:18, 19), they are involved and incorporated with Him as the 'firstborn among many brothers' (Rom. 8:29). The importance of this issue of adoption into God's family, with as its badge the right to call God 'Abba', is expressed by Joachim Jeremias, who wrote a book on this theme, entitled *The Central Message of the New Testament*. He sets out a case that makes this four-letter word 'Abba' the heart of the Gospel. 'Abba' is one of the Aramaic fragments in the New Testament, and is a word of family intimacy, like 'daddy' in English.

(3) Believers are in Christ as their *dominating influence*. In the Roman Empire, it wasn't merely Julius Caesar who 'bestrode the narrow world like a Colossus' as Shakespeare's play says. The promotion of Emperor worship by Augustus as a kind of loyalty-cement meant that an individual's allegiance could be elicited by the confession 'Caesar is Lord'. To the Christian however, the highest expression of discipleship was the statement that 'Jesus is (my) Lord' (Rom. 10:9, 10). By making this good confession, believers were saying that Christ dominated their faith, their thinking, their relationships and their choices in life. It is amazing that this letter was written by a man dominated by Christ, yet a prisoner of the Roman Emperor. He was surrounded by a culture which was openly hostile to the message he proclaimed, yet is able to sense the presence of Christ where he is, in jail, and view his position as part of a set of God-given circumstances. This kind of heart outlook makes Christians in society operate in the world, to use John Stott's happy phrase, as 'a subversive counter-culture'.

Some years ago, a Wycliffe Bible Translator missionary, Des Derbyshire, was working in the north of Brazil. His best informant and first convert was the cleverest man in the tribe, the chief's son. Derbyshire was making good progress, when one day a small plane landed on the rough landing-strip, and out stepped the world statesman Bobby Kennedy (President John F. Kennedy's brother), who was interested in developing cultures. All afternoon and into the early evening, Kennedy used Des Derbyshire's translation skills to question the young man about the history and habits of the tribe, their customs and hunting skills, and the range of the activities of this people who would at that time be called 'primitives'. Finally, as the evening shadows lengthened, Kennedy told Derbyshire to ask the chief's son what he liked doing best out of the full range of tribal activity.

In that hut the young man said to the world statesman: 'I like best being occupied with Jesus.' This is the over-arching activity which characterises those who are 'in Christ'.

The reference to **overseers and deacons** in **verse 1** illustrates how church leadership was developing in the early years. It was a group, rather than an individual, responsibility. The overall care of the churches was in the early days at least an apostolic function, and the letters of Paul seemed to be shared among the churches. Because of the role of the apostles in the formation of the inspired record in the New Testament, we ought to be arguing, in the view of the present writer, not only for the uniqueness of Christ, but also for the uniqueness of the apostolic witness to Christ. Some of the self-styled 'apostles' of today's church are Lilliputians beside 'Gullivers' like Paul and Peter! The care of God's flock in a local church devolved on people involved in a two-fold role of oversight and practical care, for example for widows (see Acts 6:1-7, where the word 'deacons' is not actually used, but where a useful template for their duties is provided). There would be some overlap between the activities of overseers/bishops, and deacons. The early church leadership structures were not rigid. There was a partnership in leadership. The saints operated in partnership **with** the elders and deacons.

We would expect, at the very least, a catalogue of complaints from Paul about the restrictions of prison life, the awareness of cold stone and the hard faces of his captors, his sore bones, and dull diet. Every one of these factors would be present and relevant, but the response we are given is refreshingly different. It is remarkable that he is keen and able to write at all. He replaces the normal method of greeting in secular letter-writing with a 'desire transfer' of essentially Greek and Hebrew blessings: **Grace and peace to you**.

Grace is a sunshine word. **Grace** is free, unmerited, undeserved and unearned favour from God (Eph. 2:8, 9). It has around it a halo of beauty, emanating from a generous-hearted God. In the Roman world, it signified the Emperor's bounty as he distributed largesse on his accession or birthday. In a Christian sense, it is God's gift of eternal life mediated through the self-giving of Christ on the Cross (Rom. 6:23). The old acrostic for Grace was '**G**od's **R**iches **A**t **C**hrist's **E**xpense.'

The **peace** mentioned here is not merely the conventional Hebrew greeting 'shalom' used by passers-by on the street. It is Christ's positive gift to anyone who has experienced the spiritual blessing of a heart at ease with God through sins repented of and forgiven. It is best epitomised in the words of the Lord Jesus Christ 'Peace I leave with you; my peace I give you. I do not give to you as the world gives. Do not let your heart be troubled, and do not be afraid' (John 14:27). We live in a world which robs people of peace and fills them with dis-ease. The cut-throat rat-race of modern life has made worriers of us all. Britain has at this time become a nation of insomniacs. That is why television programmes can continue all through the night – there will always be a good viewing audience of those who cannot sleep. The corrosive influences of worry about our families and our debts haunt us (we carry at least £1,000 of debt per person in our little island, not counting mortgage debt). We worry about how we are going to pay for things which advertisers or peer pressure makes us think we need to buy. We pay other people to bring up our children in the most influential and formative years of their lives, miss out on the fun of spending time with our kids, and then wonder why they feel resentful and we feel guilty. On a broader canvas, world poverty, homelessness and fear – fear of land-mines, fear of poisoned land and polluted rivers – rob people of peace. On a recent visit to Brazil, I learned how favela (shanty-town) people worry about their children. The children have to be able to read in order to be admitted to the State schools, but the parents have neither the money for the fees to pay for pre-school education, nor the time and skills to teach their own children to read. Under-nourishment stunts the growth of the children's brains, and their living environment condemns them to a cycle of failure. They dare not hope in the political system to liberate them. Their only hope is in a life-changing gospel, and in a Saviour who can bring them real peace. In a purple passage in Ephesians chapter 2, we see Peace in Person (verse 14), embodied in Christ, who is our peace; Peace in Action (verse 15) as He becomes the Peace-Maker, actively intervening for the benefit of sinners; and Peace in Proclamation (verse 17) as the peace of the Christ who never visited Ephesus is proclaimed by apostolic preaching. Essentially, He has made peace 'through the blood of His cross' (Col. 1:20).

Verses 3-11: Thanks

The basis of Paul's thankful and joyful prayer in verses 3 and 4 is the active participation of the Philippian believers in the gospel (v.5) from day one. When we fail to express thanks for the simple favours of life, it can have a chilling effect on others. The Letter to the Philippians is a model of Christian courtesy. Having thanksgiving near the top of the 'menu' in our prayers would revolutionise our praying.

The **joy** of verse three is worth some detailed consideration, for it is a valuable by-product of thankful prayer. Here is a prisoner in the iron grip of Rome, teaching us to be joyful. Joy is part of the harvest of the Holy Spirit in the life of Christians (Gal. 5:22), a quality grounded in God rather than an emotion based on human feelings. Joy was a 'trade-mark' of the early church (Acts 2:46; 8:8; 13:52;

41

15:3). In Philippians, it transcends contention (1:18), fuels confidence in God's delivering power (1:18b, 19), accompanies spiritual growth (1:25), deepens fellowship when Christians are reunited (1:26), is fostered by believing unity (2:2), accompanies sacrificial service (2:17,18), enhances a Christian welcome (2:29), reinforces sound teaching (3:1), characterises Christian stability (4:1), bears repetition (4:4), and motivates Christian giving (4:10). A. T. Robertson defines Paul's joyful prayer life in this letter as 'a spiritual rhapsody'.

Their human **partnership** or 'koinonia' **(v.5)** in the Gospel 'from the first day' is matched in **verse 6** by divine **preservation.** This is one of the bedrock statements of the whole letter. Paul finds himself in a context of hostility, not only from a pagan State, but from antagonistic fellow-believers. Nevertheless, he is aware that there is a fundamental work of God going on in Philippi, and that it is a work rooted in the lives of the Christian people he knows, and those who have come to faith since he last saw them. Their fellowship in faith and grace, in prayer, loving support, service and mission, are matched by God's activities on their behalf. God is the Initiator of every good work, in creation and society and Christian living. Paul recognises here how prodigal and indiscriminate God is in His generosity to godly and ungodly alike. Paul didn't start it, and the Philippians didn't start it as some sort of self-improvement measure.

The **good work** is a good work of God's grace, encapsulated principally in two areas of activity – salvation (Christ's work for us) and sanctification (the Holy Spirit's work in us). The term 'He who began' (*enarchamenos*) denotes that God began it, as its source or fountainhead in a decisive inauguration. This good work is also His **consistent pattern**. The same sovereign Lord observes a

careful persistence in continuing the work. God is not a 'Quitter'. He is not like the man our Lord spoke about in Luke 14:28-30, who began a tower without counting the cost, and then was mocked for failing to finish it. God sees things through in our lives. Paul is able to give a **confident promise**: 'Being confident of this ... that God will bring the work to completion' (*epitelesei* = 'bring to completion', is related to the word *telos*, meaning 'goal' or 'target'). Paul's confidence in their perseverance is not based on his convictions about their inherent strength of purpose or good practice as Christians, but on the One who started it all, and who will see it through when their self-giving to God is completed in death (Heb. 12:23), and beyond. Sometimes we are downhearted when we reflect on our failure to match up to even our own low targets in life. We make resolutions about saving or slimming, we make spiritual promises to ourselves about our prayer life or our stewardship of God's money, and we are tempted to give up, or at least to opt out of Christian activity. Here, the apostle encourages us to think of ourselves as people in whose lives God is at work. Something useful and permanent is going on here!

> The work which His goodness began,
> the arm of His strength will complete,
> His promise is Yea and Amen,
> and never was forfeited yet;
> Yes, I to the end shall endure,
> as sure as the earnest is given,
> More blessed, but not more secure,
> the glorified spirits in heaven.

There will be an intermediate and a final fulfilment of God's purposes in us. The Day of Christ Jesus is also called 'The day of Christ' (Phil. 1:10; 2:16), 'the day of our Lord Jesus (Christ) (1 Cor. 1:8), the day of the Lord (1 Thess. 5:2; 2 Thess. 2:2), 'the day' (1 Thess. 5:4), and 'that day' (2

Thess. 1:10). The intermediate fulfilment occurs when we die, and are 'away from the body, and at home with the Lord' (2 Cor. 5:8). The ultimate fulfilment will take place when at Christ's Second Coming our souls shall be reunited with refurbished bodies (Phil. 3:21), equipped for praise for all eternity, when the full number of Christ's Bride, the church on earth, is complete. We will be united with Him as the Bridegroom, and every human being will witness or experience His vindication in judgement. What a Day that will be!

In **verse 7,** Paul proves that his attitude to the Philippian believers is not merely one of emotional attachment. His warm-hearted love for them is a morally right attitude for any fellow-believer, and he is pleased to notice that they share with him in God's grace **and** in his state of captivity as an extension of their mutual sharing in God's keeping power.

Verse 8 continues in a serious and warm-hearted way. His words are not to be taken lightly, since 'God can testify' (see Romans 1:9; 2 Corinthians 1:23) about his intense longing (the 'epi' of the verbal form *epipotho* strengthens its meaning, see Romans 1:11; 1 Thessalonians 3:6), which he links with the 'affection' (*splanchnoi*), or viscera of Christ. The verb *splanchnizomai* means 'to be moved with compassion', and is used of the Lord Jesus in the Gospels (e.g. Matt. 9:36; 14:14; 15:32; 20:34), of the Master's pity (Matt. 18:27), and of the Father in the parable of the Lost Son (Luke 15:15, 20). The language seems to regard the stomach area as having a brain and feelings of its own. The verb portrays the reality of the Lord Jesus' 'gut reaction' to human need, and usually results in self-giving action. Jesus teaches the crowd, or touches the leper, or feeds the hungry. I once heard a lady student pray, 'Lord, please blow up our refrigerators, and install some heating elements!'

Verses 9-11 set out one of the distinctives of Christian life and experience – a life of prayer. Prayer is an unnatural activity for the self-sufficient, because when we pray we are going outside of ourselves for help. The grace of God experienced in the gospel makes us aware of the need for prayer. When Rev Andrew McBeath, Principal of the Bible Training Institute in Glasgow (now part of the International Christian College), was a student at New College, Edinburgh, a student asked a lecturer why lectures started with prayer, and examinations didn't. The answer given was that outside help was not permitted in examinations. For the Christian, outside help is always needed in examinations. Prayer is not simply words, like a shopping list for the celestial super-market. Prayer is also adoration, basking in the love of God. In a sanatorium, they used to wheel out the beds of tuber-culosis patients into the sunshine, to benefit from its healing rays. Prayer also has a corrective influence in our lives. Firstly, a Christian with a tender conscience knows that there should be some sort of match-up between what we pray and how we live. Dr Arthur Wright, a gold medallist in medicine who chose to serve Christ for over thirty years in a village in Congo, said: 'You cannot pray the prayer unless you live the life.' Secondly, prayer can transform relationships. It is harder to be harsh and critical of others when we have been praying for them. In verses 9-11, Paul's expression of thanks ignites into prayer for them in five ways:

1. A multiplication of love (verse 9a) which will lead to
2. An expansion of spiritual perception (verse 9b)
3. Heightened powers of discernment (verse 10a)
4. A purified character (verse 10b), and
5. A personality rounded with righteousness (verse 11a).

45

1. A Multiplication of Love.

Their **love** in verse 9 is *agape*, not our overworked word, but one of four main terms used in Greek. (The others are *storgia*, which is affection, *philia*, which is brotherly or family love, and *eros*, which signifies sexual love.) *Agape* had an exclusive use in secular Greek writings for the love-relationship between the gods. It became a new coin minted on the lips of Jesus to express the love of God, now brought into the market-place of life, and to express the relationship now existing among God's children (see Ephesians 4:32–5:2; 5:25-33). In the apostle Paul's graphic language in Romans 5:7-8, he draws out the distinctives of it: 'Very rarely will anyone die for a righteous man, though for a good man someone might possibly dare to die. But God demonstrates His own love for us in this: while we were still sinners Christ died for us.' *Agape* is a generous outpouring of divine love. In today's world, people sometimes say 'I love you' when they really mean 'I love me; I want you'. God is not like that. His overflowing generosity in the death of Christ melts the hearts of sinners who realise it. God's love is like the sun in the old story of the contest which took place between the wind and the sun, to make a man remove his coat. The harder the wind blew, the tighter the man clung on to his coat, but when the sun shone in its brilliance, off came the coat! Believers can bask together in that love, sharing its divine source in human ways, so that it may 'abound more and more'.

2. An Expansion of Spiritual Perception.

The highlighting of **knowledge** (*epignosis*) in verse 9 underlines what we mentioned in the 'Themes' section of the Introduction, namely, that Paul emphasises the Christian's mind in this letter. An experience of the regenerating and renewing work of the Holy Spirit in our lives does not mean that we have to jettison our brains! Love and knowledge are like features in the decor of a house which enhance each other. Knowledge on its own is sterile (1 Cor. 13:2). There is nothing more boring than hearing preachers whose Christianity is purely 'bookish', unrelated to life. The totally academic approach to Scripture can be merely an ego-inflating exercise – 'knowledge puffs up, love builds up' (1 Cor. 8:1) – but a real experience of the love of God, coupled with knowledge in the sense of spiritual awareness of practical need, produces a potent partnership in the relationships of the believer to God and to his fellow-believer.

3. Heightened Powers of Discernment.

Christians can be warm-hearted and well-meaning, and yet can sometimes be unwise in their decision-making, so Paul wisely throws another flavour into this pot-pourri of Christian qualities. It is the ability to display **depth of insight (verse 9)**, to show spiritual good sense (the Greek word *aisthesei*, from which we get our word 'aesthetics', occurs here only in the New Testament). This insight assesses priority as well as quality in the realm of doctrine and behaviour. In other words, our Christian love is tempered by discernment, and flows along channels lined with common sense. A new Christian I knew was so full of his new-found faith that he felt he had to share it with everyone – by working his way through the telephone directory, which was fine until the first telephone bill came in! His zeal was admirable! **Verse 10** extends the practical wisdom which Paul prays for the believers in the use of the word *dokimazein*, **able to discern**. The verb has a metallurgical background, of material approved and acceptable after testing. The writer used to work in the steel industry, where batches of freshly-made steel lay in the railway sidings until the battery of chemical and physical tests which made up the specification for that batch was satisfactorily completed. Only then could the steel go into useful service. In 1 Corinthians 16:3 and 2 Corinthians 8:22 Paul uses it of qualified men who can be trusted to take charge of money, and in Romans 12:2 of verifying God's will by practical tests. Here it is used of the Christian who under God's guidance chooses only the best. See also Philippians 4:8-9. Christian organisations are sometimes taken in by fast-talking entrepreneurs who like playing with other people's money, or by sloppy individuals who have no sense of responsibility in handling God's money. Neither of these kinds of people pass the tests set out here.

4. A Purified Character.

The word **pure**, **verse 10**, (*eilikrineis*) is accepted by most scholars as metallurgical, with the meaning unmixed, like metal from which the surface slag, containing the impurities which have emerged in the refining process, has been skimmed off. A few scholars take the word as compound, literally 'sun-judged', meaning 'able to stand sunlight'. The concept behind the term **blameless** in verse 10 (*aproskopoi*') means 'undamaged in transit', hence the idea of being 'without blame'.

5. A Personality Rounded with Righteousness.

Paul prays that the Lord will build all of these qualities into their lives as part of His process of sanctification. There is a car sticker which reads, 'Be patient – God isn't finished with me yet!' There are imperfections in all our characters and personalities. But the **fruit of righteousness** in our lives demonstrates that we are increasingly 'conforming to the norm' (the basic idea of the Old Testament word for righteousness) of the character of the Saviour we profess to follow. That will bring glory and praise to God on 'the Day of Christ' (see 1:6). The world at large is not interested in sermons or theological arguments. We have become a tabloid culture, and in the computer age we have developed an appetite for 'bytes', digested bits of information. We will not take time, nor do we have the patience, to listen to convoluted arguments. In the post-modern age, people are cynical about words which claim to express any absolute truth or objective fact. The most convincing argument for Christianity in the early centuries of its existence was the quality of living demonstrated by the followers of Jesus. Tertullian (ca. 160- ca. 220) was a converted lawyer from North Africa who became one of the father-figures of the Early Church, and a great Apologist for the faith. The summary of Tertullian's apologetic to a hostile pagan world was, 'Watch us, how we live! Watch us, how we die!' Perhaps this should be our greatest evangelistic resource today – quality Christian living, radiating a warm love for each other, and a healthy, loving interest in others, so that the church fulfils the definition given that 'it is the only society which exists for the benefit of its non-members'.

QUESTIONS FOR DISCUSSION: 1:1-11

1. What are the advantages of a letter as (a) a means of communication, and (b) a means of communicating the gospel?

2. Is being a servant of Christ the same as being a doormat for Christ? Are there any limits you can put on your understanding of the word 'servant' without destroying its essential meaning?

3. Suppose someone described one of your fellow-church members as 'a real saint'. Would it be right to object to or correct this verdict, and how would you do it?

4. In what ways can modern Christians engage in 'partnership in the gospel'? (1 verse 5)

5. How can we encourage relationships with fellow-Christians which result in 'longing', and 'affection' among us?

6. Are knowledge, insight and discernment valued among Christians today? (see 1 verse 9). If not, can you think why not? How could we improve their valuation?

3

THE CAUSE OF CHRIST
1:12–30

[12] Now I want you to know, brothers, that what has happened to me has really served to advance the gospel. [13] As a result, it has become clear throughout the whole palace guard and to everyone else that I am in chains for Christ. [14] Because of my chains, most of the brothers in the Lord have been encouraged to speak the word of God more courageously and fearlessly.

[15] It is true that some preach Christ out of envy and rivalry, but others out of goodwill. [16] The latter do so in love, knowing that I am put here for the defence of the gospel. [17] The former preach Christ out of selfish ambition, not sincerely, supposing that they can stir up trouble for me while I am in chains. [18] But what does it matter? The important thing is that in every way, whether from false motives or true, Christ is preached. And because of this I rejoice.

Yes, and I will continue to rejoice, [19] for I know that through your prayers and the help given by the Spirit of Jesus Christ, what has happened to me will turn out for my deliverance [20] I eagerly expect and hope that I will in no way be ashamed, but will have sufficient courage so that now as always Christ will be exalted in my body, whether by life or by death.

[21] For to me, to live is Christ and to die is gain. [22] If I am to go on living in the body, this will mean fruitful labour for me. Yet what shall I choose? I do not know! [23] I am torn between the two: I desire to depart and be with Christ, which is better by far; [24] but it is more necessary for you that I remain in the body. [25] Convinced of this, I know that I will remain, and I will continue with all of you for your progress and joy in the faith., [26] so that through my being with you again your joy in Christ Jesus will overflow on account of me.

[27] Whatever happens, conduct yourselves in a manner worthy of the gospel of Christ. Then, whether I come and see you or only hear about you in my absence, I will know that you stand firm in one spirit, contending as one man for the faith of the gospel [28] without being frightened in any way by those who oppose you. This is a sign to them that they will be destroyed, but that you will be saved – and that by God. [29] For it has been granted to you on behalf of Christ not only to believe on him, but also to suffer for him, [30] since you are going through the same struggle you saw I had, and now hear that I still have.

The cause of Christ has always provoked reaction from its opponents, and sometimes an unhelpfully aggressive approach from some of its doughty defenders. Some years ago, the results of a study of violent incidents from the New York police files was published. The researchers discovered that, in general, it was the same restricted number of police officers who seemed to be drawn into violent incidents. The second conclusion was that violence is usually a two-way thing, involving both the police officer and the member of the public concerned. The third discovery was that the responsibility for initiating violence usually rested on the police officer – the way he wore his uniform (particularly his hat!), his style of walking, his tone of voice and mannerisms.

Tacitus, the father-in-law of Julius Agricola the Roman governor of Britain, said in his *Annals* that Christians were 'hated for their enormities'. Paul found himself at the receiving end of Roman justice, waiting for a trial verdict, at the vortex of strong and even violent emotional responses from his fellow-Christians. For some he would be the focus and inspiration for Christian witness, and for others he would be the butt of ridicule because of his lowly position. Whatever happened, he would be used as a catalyst for conflict. Those who were 'agin' the government' would use his imprisonment as an excuse for verbal attack on Roman authority, and those who were his opponents within the Christian church would magnify themselves at his expense.

During the First World War, one of the propaganda slogans asked the question, 'Am I being offensive enough?' Some Christians have no problems being offensive to their non-Christian friends, or to their fellow-believers. For them, the 'offence of the Cross', as they would call it, transmutes into the offensiveness of the Christians! By way of contrast, Richard Wurmbrand quotes the response of one of his prison guards to the statement in Luke 24:28 that Jesus would have gone further, and waited to be invited into the Emmaus home. Wurmbrand's guard, who had suffered the incursions of a Communist State into his privacy, said, 'Oh, Jesus! You have won me by your politeness!' This section of Philippians we are about to study exposes these varied reactions. The Cause of Christ is, first of all:

Known in Restriction (1:12-14)

As he says elsewhere in this letter (3:13) Paul is single-minded in his energy output, and in his assessment of the results of his efforts. His key thought is not that of his personal safety, but of how to advance the gospel (see 1 Timothy 4:15 for Timothy's trail-blazing advance), and in verse 12 he includes his imprisonment within this overview. Discussion of the gospel raises the whole question of what the 'gospel', or 'good news' (*euangelion*) is. Bishop Taylor Smith used to say that the gospel could be summed up in three phrases.

The first phrase is 'God is', that is, an expression of belief that He exists. Hebrews 11:6 says, 'without faith it is impossible to please God, because anyone who comes to God must believe that He exists.'

The second phrase highlighted by the good bishop is 'God loves', and we could note that as a major theme, not only of John's Gospel, for example John 3:16 ('For God so loved the world that He gave His one and only Son'), but also a major theme of the first letter of John, for example, 1 John 4:7-8: 'Dear friends, let us love one another, for love comes from God. Everyone who loves has been born of God and knows God. Whoever does not love does not know God, because God is love.'

The third phrase is 'God loves me'. For an authentic

experience of the Gospel, the Holy Spirit makes us aware that the death of Christ is not just a general death for the sin of humankind, but a particular death for *my* sin. This was the kind of gospel awareness which stopped Paul in his tracks as he went on a persecuting 'witch-hunt' to Damascus. He thought that he was persecuting the Christians, but discovered that day that he had been persecuting the Christ (Acts 9:5: 'I am Jesus, whom you are persecuting'). This blaspheming ex-persecutor could never forget God's goodness and grace shown to him. He expresses it in Galatians 2:20: 'I have been crucified with Christ and I no longer live, but Christ lives in me. The life I live in the body, I live by faith in the Son of God, *who loved me and gave Himself for me.*' This surging new life given by God changes our whole attitude to worship, the Bible, prayer and Christian service. The Good News of Jesus Christ becomes the focus and fulcrum of our living.

What is at the heart of this gospel? Most scholars would concede that 1 Corinthians 15:3-4 provides a seminal, Early Church, summary of what the gospel is. 'For what I received I passed on to you as of first importance: that Christ died for our sins according to the Scriptures, that he was buried, that he was raised on the third day according to the Scriptures.'

This gospel made the church, and churches live or die in relationship to their faithfulness to the gospel. Some scholars put the cart before the horse, and say that the reverse is the case – it was the church that manufactured the gospel. They would regard much of the material we have in the gospels as a group invention. The gospels then become an amalgam of teaching stories produced in separate forms by the group dynamic of a consensus of believers, each one with a 'punch-line' summary of the teaching, like Mark 2:27-28: 'The Sabbath was made for man, not man for the Sabbath.

So the Son of Man is Lord even of the Sabbath.'

If we are looking for a sensible summary of the gospel, we can do no better than consider 1 Corinthians 15:1-8, the gospel is, first of all, *a Spirit-given Story*. It is *shared truth* (see verses 1 and 3), a sacred deposit of living experience passed on down the generations. It is *solid truth* – a basis on which to lean (hold firmly), and a belief by which to live (see verse 2b, 'otherwise, you have believed in vain'). It is *supreme truth*, priority material ('of first importance', verse 3). It is not merely a life-and-death issue, it is a life-and-death-and-resurrection issue. This word or corpus or body of truth is God's living, inspired Word, surging with dynamic life.

The gospel is, secondly, *a Self-giving Sequence.* In the gospel, Christ gives Himself to us and for us. The gospel is *centred on a Person*, and the total package of, or sequence of, His death, burial and resurrection (verses 3 and 4), what some theologians call 'the Christ-event'. 'Christianity is Christ' is not an empty slogan. The gospel is *focussed on an action.* The phrase 'Christ died for our sins' is neither exclusively historical, related merely to facts, nor exclusively personal, related only to values. It is a valuation of the facts. The fact of Christ's death can be verified outside of the New Testament, for example in Tacitus' *Annals* (dated around A.D. 115), which is one of the earliest witnesses in non-Christian literature to the crucifixion. Paul's valuation and extension of this fact highlights Christ's self-giving, dealing in His death with the basic problem of our sins – alienation in relation to God, bondage in relation to ourselves, and conflict in relation to others. The gospel actually reverses the human order of 'me first, others second, God last', and restores the Divine order of 'God first, others second, myself last'.

The gospel is, thirdly, *A Saving Spectacle.* The word

'appear' (*ophthe*) occurs four times in fact and a further twice by implication, in **verses 5-8.** This highlights the importance of *vision* in our lives. The Philippian church was actually born by means of a vision (Acts 16:9). The great vision of our lives is when we look to the Lord Jesus Christ in a saving way (see Numbers 21:9; John 3:14-15). We need to do what John the Baptist told his hearers to do: 'Look! The Lamb of God, who takes away the sin of the world.' James Baldwin, the Civil Rights activist, said: 'Those who are possessed by a vision do not so much follow it, as find themselves driven by it. Otherwise they could never endure, much less embrace, the lives they are compelled to lead.' The hymn-writer says:

'Since my eyes were fixed on Jesus,
I've lost sight of all beside,
so enchained my spirit's vision,
gazing at the Crucified'.

This gospel, and this Lord Jesus Christ, were the motivating forces which kept Paul the prisoner 'on track'.

The gospel can reach anywhere, even into a Roman guardhouse. Acts 28:20 portrays Paul as constantly chained to a Roman soldier, and in Ephesians 3:1 he calls himself 'the prisoner of Christ'. The 'palace guard' (*praitoreo*) in **verse 13** is the Greek rendering of the Latin 'praetorium' and refers primarily to the detachment of troops which formed the Emperor's bodyguard, and secondarily to their barracks, or living quarters, so that it is possible to have a praetorium in Jerusalem (Mark 15:16; Matt. 27:27; John 18:28), Caesarea (Acts 23:35), or Rome, if, as we have said in the introduction, Philippians was written there (see also 4:22 for the reference to 'those who belong to Caesar's household'). Shift-workers can be notorious talkers (it whiles away the time), and we can visualise this celebrity prisoner becoming a topic of conversation as the guard was changed. Paul would relish the challenge of the gospel and the Lord Jesus being talked about in Rome. Verse 14 makes it clear that the Christians in Rome were given a fresh impetus to witness. Courage is contagious. This was sorely needed for a group which Tacitus says were 'hated for their enormities' (Christians were accused of idolatry because they had no visible representation of their God, of immorality because of the unhealthily close relationship between 'brothers and sisters', and of cannibalism because the pagans had heard that Christians 'ate the flesh and drank the blood of the son of man'). Paul's arrival and open testimony inspired his fellow-believers to be bold and fearless in their witness. There have always been dodgers and cowards who slope off when danger threatens. Paul's boldness helped the Good News to be spread despite restriction. As to the content of the Good News, in the New Testament era, the church was already formulating summaries of Christian doctrine (1 Cor. 15:1ff.). There, the gospel is regarded as a Spirit-given Story. The content is passed on like a sacred deposit, across the generations. It is:

Preached in Contention (1:15-20)

In these verses, Paul switches his attention from the spread of the Good News among the soldiers, and the Christians who have been freshly galvanised into action, to those who are honest-to-goodness preachers with less-than-honest motives. They fall into two categories.

First of all, there are those who preach Christ out of envy (verse 15, *dia phthonon*) or rivalry (*erin*). Some of these preachers had perhaps lost some kudos or credence since Paul's arrival in Rome, hence the envy, rivalry and 'selfish ambition' (v.17, *eritheia*) and insincerity (v.17, *ouch hagnos*) behind their preaching. Whitefield and Wesley were divided in doctrine, but retained great love and respect for each other. Howell Harris was occasionally arrogant and Evan Roberts could be headstrong and lacking in common sense. There are always people who enjoy playing 'puncture the preacher'. Some of us have met other kinds who are Christ's mercenary soldiers, whose eyes sparkle when they see the glint of anything resembling money. Others ask the vital two questions (for them), apart from 'does it increase my bank balance?', namely, 'does it advance my career?' or 'does it enhance my status?' They love the prominence of the platform, as well as the rustle of the bank-notes and cheque-books. They are the spiritual descendants of Diotrephes (3 John 9) who 'loves to be first'. Some preachers are so unbearably proud that they find it difficult to sit in a congregation under the ministry of the Word from others. They prefer the long-term, self-inflicted punishment of listening to themselves all the time!

Secondly, there are those who preach Christ out of goodwill (v.15, *eudokia*), motivated by love (v.16, *agape*). They recognised the call and grace of God on Paul's life, and the link between the man and his message, as one which characterised their own preaching. They stood beside him as partners in defending the gospel. Encouragement is infectious in Christian service. It functions like the oxygen of the soul.

The other approach highlighted the contentious nature of the gospel as the divider of men. The Lord Jesus claimed to have 'brought a sword' when He came. Paul said the gospel was foolishness to those who were perishing (1 Cor. 1:18). The hearers would in general be unaware of the context against which the gospel was being preached, so Paul is able to rejoice (verse 18) despite personal friction. He is able to fly above the temptation to criticise others, or gossip to the soldiers. He is able to 'stay sweet', and remember his priorities. He was fully aware of the context against which the gospel developed, and the young church grew. It was not an irreligious world. On the contrary, people had a wide choice of options, ranging from the modified Greek philosophy option made palatable for theatre-goers, to the rigid rules for initiation and advance set out in Mithraism, one of the mystery religions which was a popular choice of Roman soldiers. Acts 17 illustrates the multiplicity of the gods worshipped. One wag suggested it was easier to meet a god in Athens than it was to meet a man! Little wonder that the Christian church would attract some 'camp-followers' and religious power-brokers would infiltrate the Christian church, and by their influence dilute the gospel.

It is the same in today's church, and its social context. Outside the church, tolerance is the key word. It is okay to be 'spiritual', but you mustn't say your spirituality has anything normative or unique or authoritative about it. Some of the worst enemies of the gospel are like the Trojan Horse, inside the church, an endangering and threatening presence. As it was in the days of Paul, there is a present-day need for people to defend the gospel against false brethren whose insidious attacks vary in their approach. Evangelical Christians within the church who insist on the authority of an inspired revelation in Scripture are marginalised. Those who insist that Jesus is not on a 'level playing-field' with the leaders of other world religions are regarded as freaks. Those who talk about sin and the need for salvation are regarded as haunted souls. Those who say they look forward to the return of Christ are branded as 'space-cadets', and troublemakers.

In verse 19, Paul stresses his inner conviction of a good outcome from his troubles. *Oida* ('I know') indicates full inner perception arising from observation and experience, so that the cerebral dimension is again important in thinking 'Christianly'. The supporting elements here are, on a human level, the Philippians' prayers, and on the divine dimension, the full and balanced help of the Holy Spirit. The Spirit is always 'the Spirit of Christ Jesus' since His basic function is to witness to Christ (John 16:14). His supporting work is illustrated in verse 19 by the use of the word *epichoregias* (NIV 'help'). A word which is a member of the same family is used in 2 Peter 1:5, translated 'add' in NIV and 'furnish' or 'supplement' elsewhere. In 2 Corinthians 9:10 it is used of someone supplying seed. This supplementary support given by the Holy Spirit will be like a ligament supporting a bone, or a city benefactor providing the resources for a full and balanced choir to assist in a theatrical production. We might imagine, in today's world, some football manager being bankrolled by big business to buy a successful team stuffed with powerful and skilful players. Paul's hope (see verse 20) is not based on brash confidence, but on the inner work of the Holy Spirit revealing that Christ will be exalted in him, in any physical state, in life or in death. The gospel is, secondly:

Embodied in Expectation (1:21-30)

The thought of verse 20 flows sweetly into verse 21: **For to me to live is Christ**. Here is the Christ-intoxicated man, giving an unashamed testimony which separates him from the kind of preachers he has been writing about. This is holy ground, one of the great sentences in this letter. Here the veteran missionary apostle sets out his stall for this life, and for the life that is to come. The overall impression, that of seeing life defined in terms of Christ's presence and influence, is overwhelming. A respect for the inspiration of the details of the text only serves to heighten our wonder at this terse expression of Christian living and Christian experience. The word order is emphatic in the Greek text: *emoi gar* ('for to me', that is, 'here is how I see it') and the neat enclosures of the infinitive *zon* ('to live') between the article 'the' and the article-free 'Christos', and the infinitive *apothanein* ('to die') enclosed between the article *to* and the noun *kerdos* ('gain'). There is a contrast between the present infinitive 'to live' (which underlines the process of consistent, everyday living), and the aorist infinitive 'the to die' (which underlines the act of dying, or the momentary experience of death as an isolated event). A rough rendering would be, 'For **to me** the to live (is) Christ, and the to die (is) an advantage'. The absence of the definite article with 'Christos' almost puts it in apposition to the articular infinitive 'the to live', so that the term 'Christ' functions like an adjective, defining life in terms of Christ's presence and enabling. The Lord Jesus fills Paul's horizons. If anyone wants to investigate Paul's boundary lines and parameters as a person – simple! Whatever edge you push him to, you will find Christ there! For him, life is not the irresponsible pastime of the lotus-eater or the pleasure-seeker. Nor is it the grim determination to triumph over circumstances, with his teeth gritted. Paul is neither fatalist nor cynic.

In Bruce Kenrick's 'Come Out the Wilderness', a doorstep critic of Christianity says, 'It's all right you guys talking about life – we've got to live it'. Christianity is about living. The Bible addresses the problem of practical daily living. If we believe in the inspiration of Scripture, we weigh every word in passages like this. There is a parallel in the life/death concepts here as well as a contrast. We have noted the contrast in the tenses used to render the infinitives 'to live' and 'to die'. The parallel comes in the two phrases in juxta-position: 'to live is Christ/to die is gain'. For Paul, Christ is the strength of his life (Phil. 4:13; Gal. 2:20).

Most of us mention death in terms of a 'sad loss', or similar phrase. Only a Christian outlook can view death as a gain, a benefit resulting from being freed from sin and misery, like cashing in the principal and the interest. Even in expressions of the pagan writers, death can be viewed advantageously only in the negative terms of deliverance from the burdens of living. One of the most convincing, winning features of Christian testimony in the period of the Early Church was the Christian approach to death. As we said earlier, Tertullian invited the pagans to watch how Christians live, and how they die. This would cover the violent death of martyrdom in the Roman arena during the Emperor Nero's persecution, or the steadfast testimony at the stake of the aged Polycarp, bishop of Smyrna, regarding Jesus his Saviour: 'Eighty-six years have I served Him, and He did me no wrong. How can I thus deny the One who gave me life?'

Physical death would be advantageous for Paul, because he would be united with his Lord (verse 23). In 2 Corinthians 5:8 he writes 'We are confident, I say, and would prefer to be away from the body and at home with the Lord.' His powers to praise and glorify Christ would be enhanced beyond death (1 Corinthians 13:12: 'Now we see but a poor reflection as in a mirror; then we shall see face to face. Now I know in part; then I shall know fully, even as I am fully known').

In **verses 22 and 23**, Paul's thought is oscillating between life or death as the more preferable option for him, and then in **verses 24 to 26** he sets out the clearly preferable option for them. He wants to march in step with them as they grow in grace, knowledge, fruitfulness, obedience, and a joyful faith (1:9, 11; 2:12), which will be stimulated when Paul is reunited with the Philippian believers. Paul's release after trial will result in an advance in fruitfulness in Christ's service, but his spiritual desire and his natural inclination is to depart (*analusai*), like a pilgrim striking camp, or a sailor loosening the cable of a ship, and to be ushered into Christ's nearer presence. This is 'by far and away the better thing'. It is difficult to translate the triple comparative (*pollo mallon kreisson*). **Verse 25** indicates a strong resolution of his genuine inner conflict in favour of staying. One of the great outcomes of Christian experience is Christian companionship.

Since he is staying, he urges them, 'whatever happens', **verse 27,** to conduct themselves, that is, live, as citizens of heaven (*politeuesthe*), with their feet planted firmly on earth, just as the colonists of Philippi have to live out *at Philippi*, the realities of their Roman privileges. For the Christian believers, this means that their behaviour has to be shaped by the gospel, and has to be appropriate for those who are part of Christ's kingdom. Christian conduct is the inevitable fruit of the Christian experience of God's grace. It is not a matter of the imposition of a written code. It is correct that you cannot change people by Act of Parliament, nor even by the Ten Commandments. What has happened in Christian experience is that the moral law of God has become internalised in what the old Puritans used to call 'gospel obedience'. 'What the law was powerless to do in that it was weakened by the sinful nature, God did by sending his own Son in the likeness of sinful man to be a sin offering, and so he condemned sin in sinful man, in order that the righteous requirements of the law might be fully met in us, who do not live according to the sinful nature but according to the Spirit' (Rom. 8:3-4). One of the tests of a good classroom teacher was the behaviour of the pupils when for any reason the teacher is out of the room. It will soon become apparent whether the teacher's discipline is an external imposition of authority, or whether that discipline has become internalised so that it shows in the children's behaviour. The internalising of God's law is a common factor in the lives of Christians, and would also transform the lives of the Philippian believers. Their reputation for stable Christian living will spread and Paul will hear about it. 'Noblesse oblige' summarises the expected outcome of grace-filled living from those who have experienced God's grace. It is rather like Lord Nelson's reputed signal at the Battle of Trafalgar, 'England expects every man to do his duty.' He was not spelling out the duties in detail. He anticipated that whatever crisis arose in the battle, each sailor would respond worthily. Similarly, Christians are to play their part at Philippi in a manner which is 'worthy of the gospel of Christ', or as he points out later, as colonists of heaven (see 3:20).

The word 'gospel' occurs twice in **verse 27,** and six times in the chapter. The gospel is the good news of God's deliverance, coming to those who need it most, from the One who loves them best (see Luke 4:18: 'The Spirit of the Lord is on me, because He anointed me to preach good news to the poor.' See also Isaiah 53:1; 61:1). It is a message of God's intervention to bring justice and healing and forgiveness, and salvation (Romans 1:16: 'I am not ashamed of the gospel, because it is the power of God for the salvation of everyone who believes'). The Early Church was in no doubt about its identification of God's Messiah in relation to the Lord Jesus Christ as the fulfilment of the Suffering Servant in Isaiah 53. When Philip was asked by the Ethiopian official to identify the mysterious figure in Isaiah's Servant Songs, 'then Philip began with that very passage of Scripture, and told him the good news about Jesus' (Acts 8:35).

The radical impact of the Good News puts courage into believers (**verse 28a**), so that they can stand up to the stiffest examination of their faith by way of affliction or persecution. They must not be 'frightened', like a startled horse or a scared bird. The early Christians had to face the rage of their persecuters (Acts 9:1), and the struggle continues. Christians are born into battle. It has been calculated that there were more martyrdoms in the twentieth century than in any other century in human history. Persecutors can be confronted with clear evidence of brave Christian living, yet reject the Christ who inspires it.

In **verses 29** and **30,** Paul and the Philippians share in the solidarity of suffering. We are at least able to show each other some of our scars. Christian courage is constantly shored up by suffering, and by knowing that we follow a Saviour who suffered. Hebrews 2:10 says: 'In bringing many sons to glory, it was fitting that God, for whom and through whom everything exists, should make the author of their salvation perfect through suffering.' The writer to the Hebrews says later (verse 18) in relation to a specific kind of suffering: 'Because he himself suffered when he was tempted. He is able to help those who are being tempted.' All this had of course been predicted, centuries earlier, in the prophecy of Isaiah: 'See, I have refined you, though not as silver; I have tested you in the furnace of affliction' (48:10).

QUESTIONS FOR DISCUSSION

1. How would you explain and define what is essential to 'the gospel' (v.16)? Are there features which people say are essential which you think of as non-essential?

2. Where does honest disagreement end and troublesome rivalry begin in our presentation of Christ's gospel (vv.15-17)? Can you draw any boundary lines?

3. Does the end justify the means in evangelical work (v.18)? How do our conclusions about this issue affect our strategy?

4. See verse 19. How does the Holy Spirit (here 'the Spirit of Jesus Christ') help us in our Christian lives?

5. Discuss varying attitudes to death, Christian and non-Christian. Is Paul's conclusion in verse 21 ('to die is gain') normal? Should it be?

6. Verse 25 talks about 'progress'. Can you pinpoint any growth areas in God's church overseas?

7. Do you think that Paul's statement that 'you will be saved' in verse 28 is a suitable one for our experience of salvation? What other terms do people use to describe conversion/ salvation, and how do you rate them?

8. Can you give any examples of Christians 'suffering' and 'struggling' in today's world? (vv.29 and 30).

4

THE CONDESCENSION OF CHRIST, PHASE ONE
2:1–11

If you have any encouragement from being united with Christ, if any comfort from his love, if any fellowship with the Spirit, if any tenderness and compassion, [2] then make my joy complete by being like-minded, having the same love, being one in spirit and purpose. [3] Do nothing out of selfish ambition or vain conceit, but in humility consider others better than yourselves. [4] Each of you should look not only to your own interests, but also to the interests of others.

[5] Your attitude should be the same as that of Christ Jesus:

[6] Who, being in very nature God,
did not consider equality with God something to be grasped,
[7] but made himself nothing,
taking the very nature of a servant,
being made in human likeness.
[8] And being found in appearance as a man,
he humbled himself
and became obedient to death – even death on a cross!
[9] Therefore God exalted him to the highest place
and gave him the name that is above every name,
[10] that at the name of Jesus every knee should bow,
in heaven and on earth and under the earth,
[11] and every tongue confess that Jesus Christ is Lord,
to the glory of God the Father.

The Call to Humility (2:1-4)

In the first chapter of the letter, Paul has made it abundantly clear that his joy as a Christian persists through any crisis-ridden set of circumstances. Whether he is in prison waiting for a trial verdict, or facing contention or opposition or suffering, his joy in the Lord remains intact. In this chapter, Paul is addressing the church division which is present potentially in disagreement between church members. He returns to this theme in a more specific way in 4:2. The checks and balances of Christian living operate in such a way that the Christians who are strongest on doctrine tend to be the weakest on ethics. The writer knew two ladies who had a fight in the street after attending a prayer meeting during the Week of Prayer for Christian Unity!

Paul had perhaps heard rumours about strife in Philippi and so he reminds the believers of the qualities which oil the wheels of unity, using the attention-grabbing 'If' in **verse 1,** as if the conditions had been met, or each of the qualities mentioned were really present among the believers. In **verses 2-4** the apostle links their behaviour with his own continuing joy, gives them strong incentives to operate against pride and self-interest, and then in **verses 5-11** takes them to the heart of Christ's gospel embodied in Christ Himself, and expressed in His self-emptying, selfless humility. The whole passage evokes echoes of gospel themes culled from Old and New Testament sources, which leave our hearts ringing. No wonder the section has been a seed-bed for Christian songs!

We should note in passing the important connection between theology, poetry and songs. We remember what we sing. The writer's memory of the French grammar we learned at school is very patchy, but he could sing you most of the French songs he was taught, word perfect (if not note perfect!). In the providence of God, every period of revival in the history of the church has been marked by an upsurge of praise expressed in song, both in the way God's people sing familiar praise, like the psalm-singing during the Lewis Revival in the mid-twentieth century, and in the hearty singing of fresh and creative songs, as in the period of the Evangelical Awakening in the eighteenth century.

This should not surprise us, for part of the evidence of the Holy Spirit's work of bringing us to life from the deadness of our sinful state is the stimulation of our minds. It is interesting that Paul's urgent call to Christians to be filled with the Spirit in Ephesians 5:18 is coupled with a requirement to 'speak to one another with psalms, hymns and spiritual songs. Sing and make music in your heart to the Lord' (5:19). Poetry has been defined as 'logic set on fire', a powerful combination of strong emotion and systematised thinking. Some think Philippians 2:6-11 was an early Christian hymn.

In this opening section (**verses 1-4**), the Apostle reinforces the call of 1:27-28 to be firm, united and courageous, with a fervent, four-fold appeal to exhibit at the head of their Christian agenda those positive qualities which have united them in Christ – Christ-centred encouragement, love-based comfort, Spirit-focussed fellowship, and sympathetic concern. There should be many shoulders to lean on in our times of trouble and testing, and we can, at the giving end of things, find ourselves involved in a wonderful ministry of support for others. Commenting on Galatians 6:2 ('Carry each other's burdens, and so fulfil the law of Christ'), Martin Luther says, 'Christians need strong shoulders and mighty bones to bear the burden.'

1. The 'encouragement' is *paraklesis* ('called-alongside-ness'), and indicates personal and inter-personal

incentives to experience and share the help and comfort which are the fruits of a life centred on the Lord Jesus.

2. The 'comfort' is *paramuthion*, and indicates that God's 'agape' love in their hearts should overflow from them, and stimulate them to practical alleviation of the burdens of others by consoling them.

3. The 'fellowship with the Spirit' (*koinonia pneumatos*) is a laminated phrase, and it is better not to separate it into either an objective or subjective genitive layer. It involves both a personal participation in the benefits of the Holy Spirit's presence, and an outgoing sharing of the reality of His presence with others, as a gift (see 2 Cor. 13:13), in a partnership in His fellowship life and blessings.

4. The 'sympathetic concern' (*splanchna kai oiktirmoi*) involves a physical reaction to the needs of others (see comment on 1:8), which is demonstrated in compassionate and merciful action.

This combination of qualities will result in united and heartfelt unity (verse 2), which would heighten the apostle's joy at their spiritual development. They would find a sweet agreement 'in spirit and purpose' (verse 2b), so that they thought in tune with each other, and a loving submission to each other in the Lord, exhibited in unselfish concern and practical help on behalf of other Christians and their interests (verse 4). They would therefore cultivate a symphony of the spirit, derived from the Spirit, which stands in the greatest possible contrast to the discordant cacophony of self-interest which characterises life generally. We

73

humans seem to have an inexhaustible talent for strife, division and the promotion of self through warfare. This gruesome talent was described in the pungent prose of Jonathan Swift, as Gulliver explained to his master in the Land of the Houyhnhnms the 'usual causes or motives that made one country go to war with another'.

'Differences in opinions hath cost many millions of lives – for instance, whether flesh be bread or bread be flesh; whether the juice of a certain berry be blood or wine ... whether it be better to kiss a post or throw it into the fire; what is the best colour for a coat – whether black, white, red or grey .... Sometimes our neighbours want the things which we have, or have the things which we want, and we both fight till they take ours or give us theirs. It is a very justifiable cause of war to invade a country after the people have been wasted by famine, destroyed by pestilence, or embroiled by factions among themselves ... and to set forth the valour of my own dear countrymen I assured him that I had seen them blow up a hundred enemies at once in a siege, and as many in a ship, and beheld the dead bodies come down in pieces from the clouds, to the great diversion of the spectators.'

In another part of *Gulliver's Travels*, the King of Brobdingnag says: 'I cannot but conclude the bulk of your natives to be the most pernicious race of little odious vermin that Nature ever suffered to crawl upon the surface of the earth.' Swift is in general reproducing the biblical verdict that 'all have sinned and come short of the glory of God' (Rom. 3:23). The human propensity for strife is seen in society generally. In a recent television series called *Neighbours From Hell* the broadcasters drew from a wealth of documentary evidence, illustrating our inexhaustible talent for not getting along with the people thrown across our path. This spirit of 'selfish ambition and vain conceit' has no rightful place within God's church.

One of the problems that the church faces is the idealistic expectations of those who do not go to church. Their criticism seems harsh sometimes, because the church is a collection of (saved) sinners, and its leaders are imperfect people who have to live out their Christian lives in a perfection-ridden context. There are also unrealistic expectations within the church, for example, in relation to a pastor's wife, or a pastor's children. In some churches, certain families have dominated the church scene for a few decades, and the same spirit of division which characterises the struggle for status and control outside the church finds a home among God's people. In the climate and atmosphere cultivated in Philippians 2, selfish ambition and vain conceit (v.3a) are exposed for what they are, aliens in a Christ-centred culture, like weeds in God's garden.

The 'humility' or 'modesty' (*tapeinophrosune*) of **verse 3** reminds us that, in the New Testament, humility is not a grace, but a duty. In other words, it is not something God does for us, but is our reaction to Him. It is not listed in the category of the harvest of the Spirit in Galatians 5:22ff. It is the appropriate response of sinners (even redeemed sinners) to a holy God, which spills over into human and fellowship relationships. Naturally, before grace held them in its strong hands, the Jewish element of the church would import the pride of privilege, and the Gentile element the pride of culture, both of which led to a sense of superiority. Things had to be, and were, different now. A truly humble person has to 'think his way to a sober estimate of himself, based on faith' (Rom. 12:3, New English Bible). The best route to real humility is to submit to the Scriptures, and contemplate the Cross. The Bible holds up a mirror to us in our fallen sinful nature, and the realisation that the Cross was necessary for us to be saved and forgiven should knock us flat. We learn *absolute* humility only at the feet of Jesus, and we learn *relative* humility as we willingly submit to each other. This knocks the rough edges off, like the contact between pebbles on the beach when the tide rushes in and rattles them together.

The Criterion of Humility (2:5-11)

In a cameo incident in the Book of Numbers (21:4-9), God's people learned a valuable lesson. Many of the Israelites had been bitten by venomous snakes, and when they pleaded for Moses' help, sought the Lord, and was told to hoist a snake on a pole, and whoever looked at the bronze snake, lived. This seems incidental in the story of God's people, until it assumes centre stage, as it were, in Jesus' discussion with Nicodemus, a Jewish religious leader. Jesus said to him, 'Just as Moses lifted up the snake in the desert, so the Son of Man must be lifted up that everyone who believes in Him may have eternal life' (John 3:14,15).

In the New Testament, we are constantly being recalled to focus on the Lord Jesus Christ. His great work on the Cross is central in God's plan of salvation, and should be central in our thinking. Philippians 2:5-11 calls us to focus on Christ in a wonderful way. By His life and death and example, the Lord Jesus has set out a pattern for Christian behaviour.

SUMMARY THOUGHTS ON VERSES 6-11.

Verse 6: Christ Jesus had as His innate characteristic an essentially divine nature. He regarded His equality as Son with God the Father as neither to be reached out for, because it was already His, nor to be selfishly clung to as His personal prize.

Verse 7: His real humanity is seen in the self-emptying sacrifice of obviously divine qualities to assume genuinely what was essentially a servant nature. He surrendered His position at least outwardly, He surrendered prerogatives that were rightfully His, and He surrendered power in His self-denial.

Verse 8: He submitted temporarily to a human lifestyle. He submitted to every detail of the Father's plan for the redemption of sinful human beings. The glory of His character is seen in two great voluntary acts – self-humiliation and obedience to death (unlike the rest of us, for whom death is the necessary consequence of sin and penalty for our human sin). The extent of His love is seen in His voluntary submission to death on a Cross – a criminal's punishment to Romans, and anathema to Jews, because the victim came under God's curse.

Verse 9: God the Father has authenticated Christ Jesus' work by resurrection and ascension, and has granted Him the name LORD, to grace His exalted manhood.

Verses 10 and 11: The great acts of Jesus mean that His human name forms the basis for universal confession, not merely acknowledgement, of His Lordship, under grace, or under judgement. The passage which began with Christ Jesus sharing the glory of the Father, ends with human beings enhancing that glory by open confession.

In this section, Paul points to the ultimate in unselfishness, humility and self-giving, namely, our Lord Jesus Christ, who provides the bench-mark and the criterion for living. There are dimensions in which the Imitation of Christ is an impossible ethic, for even at our best we are utterly incapable of vicarious self-giving, or total obedience. In His infinite mercy, Jesus invites us to share His yoke, and to walk with Him according to the pace and pattern set by him, only too aware of our unworthiness to do so: 'Those who fain would serve Thee best are conscious most of wrong within....' The whole passage is so mind-boggling, that the writer is overwhelmed and filled with a sense of inadequacy at attempting to explain such sublime truth. It is like sending an assistant at a 'do-it-yourself' store to paint the ceiling of the Sistine Chapel. While preparing for this, I penned the following:

DOWN, BUT NOT OUT..

Oh, how can I preach of Your glory?
A glory before time began,
A glory of pure incandescence,
Before the creation of man.

Oh, how can I preach of Your splendour?
So majestic and dazzling a King,
A visage so noble and sunny,
Light for our darkness to bring.

Oh, how can I preach of Your riches?
The wealth of Your nature and worth,
The total resources of Godhead,
Beyond comprehension on earth.

Oh, how can I preach of Your pity?
Unselfishly leaving aside
Your trappings of wonder and worship,
Self-emptying Saviour and Guide.

I'd rather be faulted for failure
To fully explain Your great love,
Than to languish here, silenced by Satan,
Unblest by Your smile from above.

The dimensions in which we can follow Christ's example have from first to last to be rooted in grace and faith rather than on effort or achievement. Thus, Barclay's translation misses the target: 'Try always to have the same attitude to life as Jesus had.' As the Christian life can neither be initiated nor sustained without the energising Spirit, we have to preface any comments about following the pattern set by Christ, and set out by Paul, with the need for total dependence on the Holy Spirit to shape our attitude and Christian behaviour. We must also pay attention to the area of Christian responsibility in the light of the experience of God's grace. The two features – dependence and responsibility – belong together.

In the light of Paul's call in verses 1-4, he now shows what the prevailing attitude and mind-set should be for Christians. He uses the present (continuous) tense in verse 5: 'keep on having this mind (*phroneite*) among you, which also in Christ Jesus.' There is no verb in the second part of the verse, so we have, basically, the options of supplying some part of the verb 'to be', or of repeating the verb in the first part of the verse. The first option relates the presented mind-set to that of our Lord. Hence, the traditional 'which was also in Christ Jesus.' The second option relates the mind-set to the Christian fellowship rather than the Lord: 'Have this mind-set among yourselves which you have as those who are in Christ Jesus'. Paul seems to indicate that there is an inter-personal, settled attitude and outlook which is equally appropriate to your role as members of Christ's church. H. A. Kennedy attempted to combine the individual and corporate aspects by suggesting, 'Think this very same thing in yourself (individually) that you think in Christ Jesus (corporately).'

In verses 6-11, we have an early Christian hymn (hence R. P. Martin's book *Carmen Christi* ('a hymn to Christ' or poem). We are in debt to R. P. Martin, E. Lohmeyer, and J. F. Collange for the technical work on the assonance and rhythm of the passage, its division into strophes, the use of rare words, and the examination of the theological content. There is no doubt that the New Testament letters yield evidence of the Early Church's use of succinct summaries of Christian doctrine, often with poetic characteristics. As we noted in our introductory comments on this passage, songs are a potent teaching tool. We cannot be sure where the hymn came from. Paul may have selected it from the corpus referred to above. It may have been part of the liturgy of the Antioch Church. Passages like 1 Corinthians 13 and 2 Corinthians 12 indicate that the apostle had a soaring, mystical side to his nature, so the construction of this early Christian Hymn could have been his. A man who has spent time in jail has had time to think. Prisoners are often homespun philosophers. People who feel things very deeply are sometimes moved to translate their thoughts into poetry. The passage has become a happy hunting-ground for academic ink-spilling. It is probably right to remind ourselves that the song was not included here for merely theoretical or theological reasons. It was included for a moral, ethical and practical purpose, so that believers would live together in harmony, unity and wonder at the condescension of their Saviour.

It is interesting that negative situations in the church, here and in Colossians 1, drew out the most positive, Christ-centred response from Paul. These verses highlight the double miracle of Incarnation and Atonement in relation to the Lord Jesus Christ. When Henri Fabre, the great French naturalist, was a boy, he was out walking with his father during the searing heat of summer, and expressed concern at the ants scurrying away from them. 'How can I let them know that I mean them no harm?' he asked his dad. 'I don't see how you could do that – unless you became an ant!' was his father's reply. In a way, that is what Jesus has done for us in His Incarnation. An old children's hymn put it like this: 'Jesus, who lived above the sky, came down to be a man, and die'.

That brings us to the second miracle – Christ's work of Atonement. In the 1970s there was a performer known by his stage name Gary Glitter. As two of the long-suffering parents who endured a weekly television programme called 'Top of the Pops', we used to marvel at the outfits worn by this performer. He came on stage, to huge applause, wearing ever more outrageous high heeled boots and dazzling costumes and make-up. By way of contrast, one of the great features of the gospel is that the Lord Jesus Christ did not come to dazzle us with His glory; He came to save us by His grace. There were occasions when the glory shone through, for example, when He was transformed before a few of His disciples at the Transfiguration (Mark 9:2-3). But this was not the major theme of His life and work:

He did not come to judge the world,
He did not come to blame,
He did not only come to seek,
it was to save He came,
and when we call Him Saviour,
we call Him by His Name.

The divisions of the passage could be:
1. Christ's Unselfish Action, verse 6.
2. Christ's Servant Heart, verse 7.
3. Christ's Sacrificial Offering, verse 8.
4. Christ's Glorious Exaltation, verses 9-11.

1. Christ's Unselfish Action (verse 6)

The thought of the participle 'being ' (*huparchon*) in verse 6 is similar to that of the Greek participle 'on' in 2 Corinthians 8:9 ('though He was'), so that the concessive meaning yields the sense 'though He was first of all', or 'originally', in the 'form of God' in His existence before His birth as a baby (John 1:1, 2; Col. 1:15, 16; Heb. 1:2-3). The present participle 'being' in verse 6 contrasts with the string of aorists ('point tenses' with no time reference) which follow it. It denotes Christ's continual possession of divine identity, in contrast to the series of decisive choices which took Him to Calvary. For those who are not familiar with New Testament Greek, we can say in general that a verb in the present tense indicates continuous action, while a verb in the aorist indicates one decisive action without time reference. (In order to help to complete the story, a verb in the perfect tense indicates an action in the past which has continuing effects in the present.) The apparent distinction between 'nature' (*morphe*) in verse 6 and 'appearance' (*schema*) in verse 8 imposed no strain on Christ's credibility. There was an innate consistency between His pre-incarnate nature and his visible appearance as a man. P. T. Forsyth summed it up well when he wrote, 'In Christ we do not hear about God; we meet Him. He did not come merely to reveal God; He is God in revelation.' William Barclay said: 'He was never more than a man, but He was never less than God.'

We are on holy ground here. In His pre-incarnate life,

Christ did not regard His equality with God as an objective to extend His powers to stretch for (*harpagmos*), either for His own self-satisfaction, or for the satisfaction of extending that recognition so that human beings acknowledged it as well as angels. *Harpagmos* occurs here only in the New Testament. In secular Greek, it means 'robbery', which is strangely off-target here. If it is taken as equivalent to *harpagma*, it means 'booty' in a bad sense or 'a windfall' in a good sense. The options seem to be to take it in an active sense, like Adam the opportunist lunging at the possibility of being equal with God, or in the passive sense of retaining a privilege or prize. *Harpage* in the New Testament indicates forcible removal (see 'greed' in Matthew 23:25; 'make by force' in John 6:15; 'attacks' in John 10:12; 'confiscation' in Hebrews 10:34). The implied contrast between the first and last Adam may be the clue to our interpretation here. Christ did not regard His divine status and equality as a privilege to be held in an iron grip, nor extended in its scope. Equality with God was innately and essentially His. Yet His voluntary self-emptying is the most eloquent display of His mind-set, in relation to verse 5, and in contrast to the first Adam, who over-reached himself.

No illustration from everyday life can fully express the sublime truths here, but let me attempt something. I once watched a runner in a half-marathon who at the finishing line took the medal which had been hung around his neck, and went over to a Downs Syndrome girl, and hung his prize around her neck. In the case of the Lord Jesus, the prize was His, but He, unselfishly, went the way of obedience rather than self-assertiveness. The kind of humility Jesus showed in relation to the work of salvation is the kind of humility the believers should show in the work of achieving unity.

2. Christ's Servant Heart (verse 7)

Scholars have exercised their wits to explain verse 7, especially 'made Himself nothing" (*ekenosen*). In what ways did He empty Himself? He retained His essential nature (*morphe*) as God, but gave up, at least temporarily, His continued existence in a manner equal to God, voluntarily stripping off the outward insignia of His divine status. He was Son of God before becoming Son of Man, and continued to be after becoming Son of Man (Matt. 1:18, 23; Mark 1:11; Luke 1:32-35; 2:11).

We have to take the phrase 'He made Himself nothing' seriously, but of course we view it, as human beings, in relation to Christ's human nature. 2 Corinthians 8:9 says 'He became poor', so He gave up His riches. In what some people call 'The Real Lord's Prayer', in John 17:4,5 the Lord Jesus talks about bringing God the Father 'glory on earth by completing the work you gave me to do. And now, Father, glorify me in your presence with the glory I had with you before the world began.' In His earthly life, He gave up His heavenly glory, although it occasionally shone through (see Mark 9:2-3). He gave up some of the joy of heaven, to become 'a Man of Sorrows, and acquainted with grief' (Isa. 53:3). He gave up His omnipresence for the geographical limitations of time and place, e.g. in Nazareth. He gave up the separation from sin and misery which is part of the life of heaven. He came 'in the likeness of sinful man to be a sin offering' (Rom. 8:3). Although sin was alien to His nature, 'He became sin on our behalf' (2 Cor. 5:21). He gave up the immunity from temptation which is an axiom of deity, and would find the sin and desolation of earth a brutal intrusion into His sensitive soul. H. R. McIntosh has argued that because of the perfection of His human nature, and His heightened sensitivity to sin, His temptations were a form of exquisite torture. The writer to the Hebrews introduces the breathtakingly daring thought of a learning process for the Son of God, which must surely be part of His self-emptying. 'He learned obedience from what He suffered' (Heb. 5:8), 'taking the very nature of a servant', a person who had no rights and knew no limits. See comment on 1:1. The use of *morphe* ('very nature') again denies any idea of assuming a role, like an actor. William Hendriksen writes: 'This is great news. It is in fact astounding. He, the sovereign Master of all, becomes servant of all. And yet, He remains Master.' His self-emptying transpired not by ceasing to be what He was, but by taking on a dimension He had not known before, namely, a truly human nature. The text cannot mean 'He exchanged the form of God for the form of a servant.' Instead He took the form of a servant, while He retained the essential form of God.

His servant attitude found expression in His everyday life. In His actions, He was fulfilling all the Servant prophecies and hopes of the Old Testament (especially Isaiah 52:13 – 53:12), and yet lived in human likeness, so that to the superficial observer, the visitor to Nazareth, or the customer in its carpenter's shop, He seemed a normal man.

3. Christ's Sacrificial Offering (verse 8)

The 'appearance' (*schemati*) is the basis of our English word 'scheme', and the verb translated 'being' is *heuretheis* which bears the sense of discovery and surprise. We might therefore paraphrase as follows: 'and being found (at any time by any person) in the scheme of things as a man.' His true humanity was self-evident, but His mind-set took Him to self-humiliation, obedience and the most excruciatingly painful death, crucifixion. The statement in verse 8 that 'he humbled Himself' is not merely a repetition of the 'He made Himself nothing' in verse 7. His obedience was, of course, to God the Father's will and plan, which took his limitless love to the boundaries of death. His being 'obedient to death' marks Him out in a uniquely distinctive way.

For the rest of us, death is the reckonable and just consequence of a life of sin (Rom. 6:23). For the Lord Jesus Christ, it was a voluntary act of self-sacrifice, since He was the sinless Son of God. 'Death on a cross' was the ultimate humiliation – cut off from society (in Jesus' case, outside the city wall), stripped, beaten and impaled (in Jesus' case by ugly spikes, probably through the butt of the hand), with the possible jarring injuries caused by dislocation of the shoulders as the cross was slammed into its socket, immobilised so that the movement of the head was the only possibility of relief (see Matthew 27:39, which highlights the cruelty of the spectators at the Cross wagging their heads in callous imitation of the Lord Jesus Christ's search for physical relief by shaking His head). At the time when He yielded up His spirit, he bowed His head (John 19:30).

The victims of crucifixion had also to suffer the constant and mounting pressure on the lungs – this was the way the Master trod. A. T. Robertson says: 'Death on a cross was the lowest rung on this Jacob's ladder of which Jesus had spoken to Nathaniel' (John 1:51). The Jews had pronounced a curse on bodies hanging on a tree (Deut. 21:23), so Paul argues in Galatians 3:13 that he has been made a curse for us. We should note that the Acts preaching does not labour the detail in proclaiming the facts of our Lord's death, but prefers the terse explanation of the course of human hate: 'You killed the Author of life...' (Acts 3:15); 'Jesus ... whom you had killed by hanging Him on a tree' (Acts 5:30).

Everything was intensified beyond our imagining for Him, the Sinless One, by having to take on the spiritual burden of the world's sin, and the abandonment of the Father (Ps. 22:1; Matt. 27:46).

Athanasius, Bishop of Alexandria, was the Early Church's 'come-back man'. He was the doughty opponent of false teaching, particularly in relation to the Person of Christ, and was exiled and imprisoned many times during his life (ca. 293-373). When he was writing about the Death of Christ, he posed the question as to why the Lord Jesus should have died on a cross. He then said that crucifixion was the only death a man can die with arms outstretched. He said that Jesus died like that to invite people of all nations and all generations to come to Him.

In his letter to the Colossian church, Paul explains the work of Christ on the Cross as a victory: 'God made you alive with Christ. He forgave us all our sins, having cancelled the written code with its regulations, that was against us and that stood opposed to us; He took it away, nailing it to the cross. And having disarmed the powers and authorities, he made a public spectacle of them, triumphing over them by the cross' (Col. 2:13-15).

In 2 Corinthians 2:14, Paul writes about 'God, who always leads us in triumphal procession in Christ'. There is no doubt that Paul has in mind the victory parade granted by the Roman Emperor to a triumphant general. There were strict rules governing the granting of a triumph. There had to be a significant increase in the territory gained for the Roman Empire. Important rulers had to be overcome in the campaign or battle, and the defeated kings were dragged in chains behind the war-chariot of the general in the procession. A large number of enemy soldiers had to be killed (sometimes prisoners of war were killed to make up the number). Much valuable booty had to be captured. When we consider the work of Christ on the Cross, we can readily find points of contact with all of this. At the Cross, Jesus took on the satanic powers of darkness and defeated them. His death has extended God's kingdom in the hearts of

Gentiles and Jews. He has conquered the hearts of a people who, although in bondage to sin and hopelessness, were valuable to God. We can tell the value of a thing by how much anyone is willing to give for it. At the Cross, God gave up His Son for our salvation: 'the Righteous for the unrighteous, that He might bring you to God' (1 Pet. 3:18). What a Saviour! What a Conqueror!

4. Christ's Glorious Exaltation (verses 9-11)

God the Son humbled Himself; God the Father exalted Him, acting in a way that was consistent with what the Lord Jesus had taught (Matt. 23:12; Luke 14:11; 18:14. See also James 4:10; 1 Peter 5:6). The resurrection reversed all the human verdicts against Him. They said He didn't come down from heaven (John 6:42) – He did. They said He deceived the people (John 7:12) – He didn't. They said He was demon-possessed (John 7:20) – He wasn't. They said He was a sinner (John 9:16, 24) – He wasn't. They said His claim to be God was blasphemy (John 10:33) – It wasn't.

In this hymn, Paul demonstrates how Christ moves from the depths to the heights, and in the final acts of the drama of redemption, resurrection (1 Cor. 15:4) is followed by ascension (Mark 16:19; Acts 1:9) and session (being seated to share the throne, Eph. 1:20). As a further example of the unusual language of this poetic passage, Paul says God has 'exalted him to the highest place', and uses the verb, *huperupsosen*, which we understand better if we put it in blunter terms: 'God has hyper-exalted Him.' Compare the terms 'market' – 'super-market' – 'hyper-market' to catch the flavour of the fact that God has exalted Him far above all. This is the only time this form of the verb is used in the New Testament (see Romans 8:37, 'hyper-conquerors', for another example of Paul's liking for compound expressions, where words are intensified by prefixing a preposition). This dramatic movement is all in fulfilment of prophecy (Isa. 52:13).

Reference to 'the highest place' in **verse 9** points out that Jesus now occupies the seat at the right hand of the throne of God (Mark 16:19; Acts 2:33; 5:31; Rom. 8:34; Heb. 1:3; 12:2). As with the downward steps of His humiliation, so with the upward steps of His exaltation, we are thinking of His human nature as the theatre in which the drama unfolds. As King, He rules the universe, over the created and redeemed order, imparting to an otherwise chaotic situation the principle of kosmos, or order (Col. 1:17). He takes a position the Levitical priests, or even the High Priest, never occupied, for there were no seats included in the Tabernacle furniture, since a priest's work was never done, and he could never sit down in the presence of God. Christ's session (sitting down) is a symbol of His completed work of salvation (Heb. 8:1). His timeless priesthood is derived from a superior order – that of Melchizedek (Heb. 5:10; 7:17). He is the focus of worship in Revelation 5:6-8.

Verse 9 tells that God 'gave' (*echarisato*), i.e., in gracious generosity, 'the name which is above every name'. The inclusion of the definite article is significant – the name is distinctive, not just any name. Is the name given, the name 'Jesus' or 'Lord'? If the former, the name 'Jesus' takes on new dimensions in the light of God's vindicating and confirmatory acts. The 'Man in the glory' has carried His earthly name with Him, and God the Father has under-written it. It is more likely that the name intended is 'Lord', or better represented as 'LORD', the capital letters indicating that as a result of His great acts of grace and salvation, the sayings of Jesus in His earthly ministry (e.g. Mark 12:35-37; John 5:22, 23; 8:58) have been transmuted so that He assumes in reality the name and character of YAHWEH, the name too holy to mention. The humanity of Jesus has become absorbed and enhanced, as it links up with His deity in new echelons of glory. A. T. Robertson describes it as 'the glory of the battle-scarred hero whose scars are His crown'. Thus, the exclusive tone of Isaiah 42:8 is broadened to include the Son of God. The name YAHWEH ('LORD'), revealed initially to Moses in Exodus 3, is a name of Creation, as the One who 'causes to be what comes into existence', to use Cassuto's phrase. It is also a name of Covenant, for by it God bound Himself to Israel in an act of spontaneous and continuous love (Deut. 7:7, 8). It is also a name for Crisis, because in any situation, YAHWEH is the 'I AM' for that situation. Although every knee will bow at the name 'Jesus', the universal confession (not simply acknowledgement) will be 'Jesus Christ is Lord' (verse 11). See comment on 1:2, section (3), under the heading 'dominating influence'.

Verse 10 extends the application of Isaiah 45:23: – 'before me every knee will bow; by me every tongue will swear' – to the Person of Jesus. The homage expressed in bowing the knee and confessing with the tongue, **verse 11**, is better understood in personal terms, that is, in relation to people rather than things. The homage will be universally all-inclusive – heaven, earth and the underworld, the elect and the reprobate (see Romans 14:10, 11; Colossians 1:16 omits the underworld). The passage seems to indicate that the aim is stronger than merely being subject to him, but actively professing that the Lord Jesus Christ is all He claimed to be.

The confession that 'Jesus Christ is Lord' is the test of an authentic experience of salvation (Acts 2:36; Rom. 10:9, 10; 1 Cor. 16:22). The Christian believers made this confession as a forthright testimony to the 'crown rights of the Redeemer' in their lives. It is not merely a statement of fact, it is an ascription of glory to God evoked from hearts which have tasted that the Lord is gracious. It was not like the light-hearted assent 'Caesar is Lord' normally given throughout the Roman Empire, from the time of Augustus, who introduced veneration of the Emperor as a loose cement to bind the disparate units of the Empire. To the believers, there was 'only one Lord, Jesus Christ', and many of the first century Christians were destined to die for this belief during the persecutions of Nero and Domitian. Such enlightened confession of God the Son, who is the Light of the World, magnifies and multiplies the glory of God the Father, so that the light shines brighter.

QUESTIONS FOR DISCUSSION – 2:1-11

1. How does your church foster/display encouragement, fellowship, tenderness and compassion? (verse 1). Give examples.

2. What kind of things could be done in church life out of 'selfish ambition' or 'vain conceit'? (verse 3). What action can we take to preserve a spirit of unity in a local church?

3. In what ways does/could our church fulfil a servant role in our community?

4. Did Jesus have two natures at the same time (see verse 6 'in very nature God' and verse 7 'taking the very nature of a servant')? How would you explain this to an unbeliever?

5. Could you give examples of Jesus' humility and obedience?

6. 'Philippians 2:10-11 teaches that everyone will eventually be saved.' Do you agree? If not, how do you make sense of these verses?

5

THE CONDESCENSION OF CHRIST, PHASE TWO
2:12–30

[12] Therefore, my dear friends, as you have always obeyed – not only in my presence, but now much more in my absence – continue to work out your salvation with fear and trembling, [13] for it is God who works in you to will and to act according to His good purpose.

[14] Do everything without complaining and arguing, [15] so that you may become blameless and pure, children of God without fault in a crooked and depraved generation, in which you shine like stars in the universe [16] as you hold out the word of life – in order that I may boast on the day of Christ that I did not run or labour for nothing. [17] But even if I am being poured out like a drink offering on the sacrifice and service coming from your faith, I am glad and rejoice with all of you

[18] So you too should be glad and rejoice with me.

[19] I hope in the Lord Jesus to send Timothy to you soon, that I also may be cheered when I receive news about you. [20] I have no-one else like him, who takes a genuine interest in your welfare. [21] For everyone looks out for his own interests, not those of Jesus Christ. [22] But you know that Timothy has proved himself, because as a son with his father he has served with me in the work of the gospel. [23] I hope, therefore, to send him as soon as I see how things go with me. [24] And I am confident in the Lord that I myself will come soon.

[25] But I think it is necessary to send back to you Epaphroditus, my brother, fellow-worker and fellow-soldier, who is also your messenger, whom you sent to take care of my needs. [26] For he longs for all of you and is distressed because you heard he was ill. [27] Indeed he was ill, and almost died. But God had mercy on him, and not on him only, but also on me, to spare me sorrow upon sorrow. [28] Therefore I am all the more eager to send him, so that when you see him again you may be glad and I may have less anxiety. [29] Welcome him in the Lord with great joy, and honour men like him, [30] because he almost died for the work of Christ, risking his life to make up for the help you could not give me.

The Continuance of Humility (2:12-18)

'Therefore' in **verse 12** links up with verses 5-11 and points to the basis for continuing in the humility mode, as Christ humbled Himself and God's good-pleasure resulted, and as through Christ God the Father strengthens believers to live lives of commensurate quality. Their past habits of obeying gospel teaching set out by the apostle should lead them into similar obedience to God even in his absence (one of the tests of a good teacher is that the class continues working even when he has to leave the classroom!). **Verses 12 and 13** set out the perfect harmony between our responsibility and God's sovereignty. 'Continue to work out ... for it is God who works in you'.

Why should this section of the letter, which is after all a statement of partnership, have become a cockpit of conflict among Bible commentators ? God's teaching must percolate continually through their thinking and behaviour. Their experience of grace leads them into an educational process in which they are active participants. There are three phases to our 'salvation' – justification, sanctification and glorification. In the first phase, God receives, welcomes and forgives penitent sinners who come to Christ and believe in Him as their Saviour. Secondly, sanctification is God's on-going process of developing Christ's image and character in us, making us sequentially more holy, and fit for heaven. The third phase, glorification, when God completes His work in us by transforming our bodies as well as our spirits, means we will be equipped to spend eternity in heaven, in the presence of God. Being a Christian is not a matter of 'crashing out' on some sort of celestial sofa.

'Must I be carried to the skies
On flowery beds of ease,
While others fought to win the prize,
And sailed through bloody seas?'

In all their efforts God is their Co-Labourer. A good working partnership makes light of heavy tasks, and with God we can 'laugh at the impossible, and cry "it shall be done".'

The Christian believer's aim should synchronise with God's – perfection. There will obviously be a disparity between intention and achievement. Christians are sometimes warned against perfectionist tendencies. A far more pernicious threat to Christian living is that we settle for sin, failure and what is second-best, which is unworthy of a great God who is preparing us for heaven, and who has provided us with tremendous resources for Christian living. A regular prayer life changes us as we bring our lives nearer to God. One of the old doggerel choruses went like this:

'Twas a grand day when I was born again,
'Twas a grand day when I was born again,
'Twas a grand day when I was born again,
'Twas a grand day when I was born again.

The sins I used to do,
I do them no more,
the sins I used to do,
I do them no more,
The sins I used to do,
I do them no more,
'Twas a grand day when I was born again!

It is right to expect change as we grow in Christ, and sad when we continue to live like spiritual paupers. How sad it is that many of us are like the man who crossed the Atlantic on one of the great liners, and was living on bread-and-cheese throughout the voyage. He had not realised that the meals were included in the price of the ticket! We can aim at the very lowest, to have the perfection of a heart undivided in its loyalties. The 'fighting talk' of Ephesians 6:10-18 reminds us of the need to patiently don the whole armour of God, and stand for God against the machinations of the evil one, never forgetting that God supplied the equipment. We have to work at it, avoiding the extremes of lazy smugness and brash confidence. Martin Luther defined the situation neatly: 'Good works do not make a good man; but a good man does good works.' There is no dichotomy between genuine trust and the most energetic work. God made us to work, and there is an inherent 'shalom' in work which can make it the perfect partner of a mind at ease with God. I once heard the translation given of a picture from a Chinese calendar, which showed a team of men in a rowing-boat, rowing like mad against mountainous seas. The caption said, 'Trust God – and pull on the oars!' The latter part of **verse 12** highlights our reaction to the unlikely combination of our frailty and God's might. We live the Christian life 'with fear and trembling'. The terror of being struck down by God's law and judgement upon sin has gone. The tender fear of responding to God's wonderful grace with ingratitude in our service, or misrepresenting such a wonderful Saviour in our witness, has replaced it.

Verse 13 underlines the grace and power at work in us as we work out our salvation. Sometimes as Christians we are unaware of the effect God's presence in our lives has on other people. I have a friend who was personal secretary to a managing director of a company. She came to Christ, and eventually was changing jobs. The day she finished work, he told her that he was glad she was leaving, and he did not want her to misunderstand, for she was the best secretary he had ever had. 'The fact is, Christine, when I see the change in you, I feel guilty every time I look at you.' What he saw was God working in her life 'to will and to act according to His good pleasure', and he found the impact of that disturbing. God takes no pleasure in the death of the wicked, but He has great pleasure in the transformed lives of His people, as He sees His plan for their lives being realised. Eric Liddell, gold medallist in the 1924 Olympics, who died in a Japanese internment camp in China, testified that 'When I run, I feel His pleasure'.

Verse 14 epitomises the moaning approach (the Greek word *gongusmon* is onomatopoeic, expressing the sound of the grumblers!) and grudging attitude of unwilling believers. Sometimes the manner in which a church steward takes in a hymnbook or shuts a door betrays reluctant service! If, as Paul has just said, God is at work in us, then we must not be constantly worn out by negative energy, like 'complaining and arguing'. A ministerial colleague's heart was almost broken by a deacon's plaintive litany at any suggestion my brother made: 'Personally, I don't think that'll work.' Grudging obedience can escalate into discontent and rebellion (Exod. 4:1-13; 16:7-9, 12; Num. 16:11; 17:5, 10; John 6:41-43, 52; 1 Cor. 10:10). Dr Martyn Lloyd-Jones says 'complaining' is indicative of a lack of love, and 'arguing' is indicative of a lack of faith.

Success in avoiding this corrosive spirit leads to the *hina* clause of purpose as **verse 15** begins: 'so that' (by way of contrast) you may become blameless (*amemptoi*, like the steadfast believers before the judgement seat of Christ, in 1 Thessalonians 2:10; 5:23), and 'pure' (that is, *akeraioi*, unmixed, unlike adulterated wine, diluted milk, or metal contaminated with impurities). The 'becoming' (*genesthe*) is there to emphasise the sanctification process following the act of regeneration. The gospel call is not to 'Be what you are not' but rather to 'become (practically) what you are (positionally) in Christ'. God's work in us can make us unblemished ('without fault', v.15), like the animals which were offered, free of defects, in sacrifice (see 1 Peter 1:19 and Hebrews 9:14 in reference to Christ's perfect sacrifice).

As James Fergusson says, Christians are to 'stop the mouths of godless pagans, by living the gospel so that the pagans may fall in love with it'.

As a young Christian, I used to question the validity of 2 Chronicles 16:9: 'For the eyes of the LORD range throughout the earth to strengthen those whose hearts are fully committed to Him', on the basis that no-one fills this qualification. I now recognise that, while our performance may not match up to it, our hearts can be fully committed to him in the sense that we have an undivided allegiance to the Lord Jesus Christ as the Master of our lives. The challenging context in which lives of such quality are to be lived out is not some sanitised, ethereal cloud cuckoo-land, but 'in a crooked and depraved generation', a world of 'bent' salesmen, unscrupulous hucksters, and dishonest brokers. A man I once knew was an office manager and made up fake wage slips to deceive his wife. It was a big shock to her system to discover what he had really been earning, after his sudden death. In another dimension, the people described here are morally as well as commercially warped in word and deed, hence the term 'depraved'. There is nothing straight about them; the path they take through life is the 'dog's hind leg' route.

In the thick of all this, the standard Paul sets is that Christians should 'shine like stars in the universe' (*kosmos* has to have a wider sense here than planet earth). We are reminded of Prince Hal's speech in Henry IV Part 1: 'and like bright metal on a sullen ground, my reformation, glittering o'er my fault, shall show more goodly', although this was written on the basis of human effort rather than divine grace. The light emanating from Christian lives is, of course, reflected light from the One who is the Light of the World (contrast John 8:12 and Matthew 5:14). A child being taken into her bedroom, said, 'Switch off the darkness,

Daddy!' Light has a preliminary task of exposing the darkness, but positively, light is there to provide illumination and direction.

In **verse 16,** this quality of living is accompanied with a presentation of the 'word of life', the message of the gospel, the Good News of salvation, proclaimed as well as embodied. This word has to be 'held out' (*epechontes*, from *epecho* which in its transitive meaning conveys the sense of 'holding fast, gripping', but the intransitive mood conveys the idea of proffering, extending, or projecting). A good Christian street-sweeper, a conscientious Christian teacher, or a careful and friendly Christian housewife, are all able to function in this way. The thoughts of light and life together make for a healthy partnership of shining and sharing. Portia, in Shakespeare's 'Merchant of Venice' says:

> 'How far that little candle throws its beam.
> So shines a good deed in our naughty world.'

When the 'day of Christ' comes, Paul will be reassured that his expenditure of effort, viewed under the sweated imagery of running and labouring, was not futile ('for nothing', *kenon*). The thought echoes the imagery of the stadium in Galatians 2:2.

In **verse 17,** Paul switches to the imagery of the Temple, and describes his life like a 'drink offering' (*spendomai*), poured out beside their sacrificial (monetary) offering, and active Christian faith (Phil. 1:29). In later Judaism in the Old Testament period (Sirach 50:5), it was customary to make, with the burnt offering, an offering of wine, poured out at the foot of the altar, like the blood of the victim. The sense therefore of verse 17 is that Paul is comparing his life given in sacrifice, as a martyr prisoner, as a parallel but secondary offering beside their sacrificial 'service' (*leitourgia,* from which we get our word 'liturgy'). Paul's Christian humility is apparent here. The Philippians' faithfulness to God in the fullest sense will inspire present and future rejoicing in Paul's heart, and a mutual sharing of that joy on the part of his Philippian brothers and sisters **(verse 18)**, like a child wanting to share his happiness with his toys on Christmas morning.

Copybook Humility: Timothy/Epaphroditus (2:19-30)

Paul reveals himself in the role of planner in this section. His primary concern is to have up-to-date news about the Philippians; he is not unduly concerned about saving his own skin. In **verse 19** he veers away from his own concerns, and thinks inclusively of the Philippian Christians, and the good influence of Timothy the envoy.

Verses 18 and 19 reflect the same mutual sharing that Paul refers to in his relationships with the Roman Christians (Rom. 1:11,12). The image of Paul as a crusty old bachelor/ loner is obviously wrong. He had plenty of enemies, but rejoiced in a wide circle of good and trusted friends. This section also demonstrates incidentally that Christians like Paul and Timothy and Epaphroditus are able to live consistently as they work out their salvation in all their own idiosyncrasies and personal difficulties. Their holiness is homogeneous. After David Livingstone's death, the Africans said of him, 'He was white all through.'

Verse 20 shows how totally suitable Timothy would be as their visitor. He was young enough to be reckoned Paul's son in the faith (1 Tim. 1:2; 2 Tim. 1:2; 2:1). His friendship was close, and his concern was real. Paul knew about his Christian heritage from his mother and grandmother, and later in life he had become Paul's special assistant and partner (Rom. 16:21). As we have seen (see on Phil. 1:1),

Paul was particularly mindful of his youth (1 Tim. 4:12), his timid nature (2 Tim. 1:7, **8**. 2 Tim. 2:1) and delicate constitution (1 Tim. 5:23). Despite these distinguishing features, Timothy was in some ways an alter ego for the grizzled apostle, hence the word 'like' (*isopsuchon* = 'soul-mate') in **verse 20.** It must have been a severe wrench for the apostle, in danger and under arrest, to part with Timothy, but the need of the Philippians and the service of the Lord were higher on the agenda of Paul's thinking than his personal needs for companionship.

In **verse 21**, Paul gives a realistic summary of life in general, and here of absence of willing volunteers to undertake such a journey. In most areas of Christian service, the bulk of the work is done by the faithful few. The mission hall through which I became a Christian had an annual 'workers' tea', and one lady murmured that if it really were a workers' tea, we could hold it in the vestry. Although there were the 'faithful few', like Timothy, Titus, Luke, and Epaphroditus, Paul is expressing the disappointment that many Christian servants feel regarding some of Christ's earthly representatives who are taken up with their own affairs. Unselfishness is unusual. The number of people available to send to Philippi were either reported missing, or reported 'sick', in the sense of being unqualified to be envoys at the time Paul needed them.

Verse 22. By way of contrast, Timothy is not like that. His mettle has been tested (*dokimen* again, see comment on 1:10), and he has emerged as strong and reliable, although he is still a young man (see 1 Tim. 4:12). Paul and Timothy were like the best kind of father-and-son team, reacting sensitively and strongly to advance the gospel and serve its highest aims in the face of any crisis. Modesty has a valid place in the curriculum vitae of a servant (1 Pet. 5:3). Yet Paul believed in affirming his friends and partners in the gospel – while they were still alive! Paul would have said a hearty 'Amen' to the general sentiments expressed in the following piece of rough doggerel:

TELL HIM NOW!

More than fame and more than money
Is the comment kind and sunny,
Is the hearty, warm approval of a friend;
For it gives to life a savour,
And it makes you stronger, braver,
And it gives you heart and spirit to the end.

If he wins your praise, bestow it!
If you like him, let him know it!
Let the words of true encouragement
Be said
Do not wait till life is over,
And he's underneath the clover,
For he cannot read his tombstone when he's dead.

If with pleasure you are viewing any work a friend is doing
If you like him or you love him,
Tell him now.
Don't withhold your admiration
Till the parson reads ovation
As he lies with snow-white lilies
On his brow.

For no matter how you shout it,
He'll not really care about it,
He'll not know how many tear-drops
You have shed.
So if you think some praise is due him
Now's the time to slip it to him;
Do not wait till there's a tombstone on his head.

Verses 23 and 24 resume the thought of verse 19, that of the sending of Timothy, who will break the news of the Roman verdict to the Philippian believers. It is worth noting in passing that one of the New Testament principles in mission is 'send your best' (see Acts 13:2,3). Paul is strongly confident that he will be released (see 1:19-26; 2:17, 18). Some scholars believe that, just as in the case of the Lord Jesus Christ, the injustice perpetrated was part of God's pre-determined plan, so here the release of the apostle fulfilled the same purpose. This alone would explain the contrast between the prison conditions Paul describes in the Pastoral Letters and the situation at the end of Acts. Further, some of the situations and place-names given in the Pastoral Letters are unattested in Acts, and can be explained only by envisaging Paul's release and further missionary activity prior to a further arrest which would culminate in his death.

Verse 25 contains a description of Epaphroditus, **verses 26-28** explain the reasons for his return to Philippi, and **verses 29-30** specify the kind of welcome he should be given on his return. His name is related to the Greek goddess of love, Aphrodite, daughter of Zeus and Dione (the Roman equivalent was Venus), and means 'devoted to Aphrodite', or 'lovely'. His family's Greek connections are probably a legacy of the polis-planting policy of Alexander the Great, whereby the cities of Asia Minor became centres for the spread of Greek culture. As a lovely Christian, he certainly lived up to his name. In verse 25, Paul uses three epithets to sum up his character, and two to describe his ministry to Paul on behalf of the Philippian believers.

First of all he is a 'brother', a fellow-member of the great brotherhood of faith which Christ has initiated as its firstborn (Rom. 8:29). The term 'brother' is used more in Philippians than in any other of the letters Paul wrote as a prisoner (1:12, 14; 2:25; 3:1, 13, 17; 4:1, 8, 21). Paul and Epaphroditus are bound together in **family love.**

Secondly, he is described as a 'fellow-worker' (*sunergon*, see Apollos, Aquila and Priscilla, Aristarchus, Clement, Mark, Onesimus, Philemon, Timothy, Titus, Tychicus), linked together with Paul in **fruitful labour.** Gospel work is not an easy option for the lazy. God made us for work. Living the gospel in such a way that we model Christ before others is often an energy-sapping exercise, not because the experience of grace and the indwelling of the Holy Spirit involve us in futile imitation, but because relationships with others who do not understand our motives sometimes wear us out.

Thirdly, Epaphroditus the worker is also a warrior, and is described as a 'fellow-soldier' (*sustratioten*. The original form was probably *sunstratioten* but the letter *nu* has become assimilated into the letter *sigma*). He is Paul's partner in **fighting loyalty,** in the spiritual warfare of the good fight of faith. The enemies to be faced were physical enemies like the Judaisers and heresy-peddling charlatans, as well as the pleasure-obsessed hedonists. The spiritual enemies were the minions of Satan, the spiritual powers of the demon population of a pagan environment, what Paul calls the 'cosmic powers of this dark world' (Eph. 6:12, Barclay's translation). Alexander Whyte of Edinburgh regarded the Christian life as 'a sair fecht (painful battle) to the end, a wrastle (wrestle) through to the very last'.

The apostle then moves on to describe Epaphroditus in relation to the Philippian believers, whose messenger (*apostolon*, **verse 25**) he was, as an appointed representative of their loving interest in Paul. He brought their gift, and cared for their brother as a true minister of the gospel, functioning as a sacred servant officially set aside for a holy task (*leitourgon*, verse 25). The sending of Epaphroditus was a spiritual as well as a practical act. We have noted before that the spiritual thing to do is often the practical thing to do. He cared for Paul in exactly the way he needed at the time, and Paul was returning him to them with warm-hearted gratitude, and as bearer of the Philippian letter.

The apostle gives three reasons for the return of Epaphroditus in **verses 26-28**. Firstly, absence had 'made the heart grow fonder', and he had been intensely homesick, pining after his Philippian brothers and sisters. This had been intensified to Gethsemane proportions because they had found out about his illness, and this sensitive soul was upset because they had been upset because of him (the word *ademonon*, 'distressed', here in verse 26 is used of our Lord's anguish in Matthew 26:37 and Mark 14:33, and is translated 'troubled' there). The servants of the Lord are not exempt from illness and physical pain. Martin Luther battled against constipation all his days, and David Brainerd suffered the agonies of tuberculosis, which drove him to an early grave at the age of twenty-nine.

Secondly, in **verse 27** Paul underlines the genuineness and seriousness of Epaphroditus' illness. It was life-threatening, but God had spared him, and thereby had spared Paul the great grief which would have resulted from the death of a Christian friend. It is worth noting in passing that healing in the apostolic era did not occur in any magical or automatic way. Although God can heal anyone, He does not heal everyone, and the starter-motor of our desire, expressed in fervent prayer, has to be enmeshed into the main engine of God's holy and sovereign will. Paul came to know this in his own practical experience (2 Cor. 12:7-10). Of course, since our bodies are God's temple, we should follow good health rules, and be careful about our eating and our exercise. Studies of ministerial burnout reveal that few ministers have a leisure activity, or have regular exercise. Many do not take a day off, refusing to recognise that it is a sin to work a seven-day week. Some work above capacity and suffer as a result. Someone recently pointed out that in Japanese factories, the machines usually run at 75% capacity, and can therefore work efficiently for long periods.

What was wrong with Epaphroditus? Some would say that it is foolish to speculate, but some of us like to at least attempt it! Perhaps it was a case of physical and mental burnout after an energy-sapping journey, lavishing t.l.c. (tender loving care) on his missionary-prisoner-friend. The illness may have struck him at the hottest season of the year. His sense of weakness and inadequacy had possibly been intensified from the hostile, overtly pagan environment, and from the shock of a sensitive person like Epaphroditus seeing so-called Christians capitalising on Paul being sidelined, and 'preaching Christ out of selfish ambition' (1:17). Epaphroditus must have found the inevitably public nature of his care for Paul a great personal strain. As a humble Christian servant, he perhaps could not bear the scrutiny of the fault-finders. Christians are imperfect people living in a perfection-ridden context, and when we don't 'shape up', we can feel we have failed the Lord, or our fellow-Christians. All of this took Epaphroditus within a hairsbreadth of death, but the God he served was a God of pity, both for him and for Paul, so that the apostle might not find sorrow stockpiling for him (*lupen epi lupen*, 'sorrow upon sorrow', **verse 27**). Sick people often try to hide their pain from their loved ones in order to spare their feelings of anguish.

Thirdly, Paul shows his own eagerness to satisfy Epaphroditus' wishes, and return him to Philippi. The believers would be glad to see him. They would have a visual answer to their concerns about his health when they saw him in person, and he would be able to thank them personally on Paul's behalf for all their kindness. This would give the

107

apostle a sense of relief (**verse 28**). See also 2 Corinthians 11:29.

In **verses 29 and 30** Paul calls for a joyful welcome home coupled to a healthy respect for a risk-taker (*paraboleusamenos*, i.e., someone who throws down their life with unselfish abandon), indicating that he has in mind others ('men like him') as well as Epaphroditus, in this category. He had thrown his life down in a gamble of the utmost self-sacrifice, as part of his work for Christ. These are the kind of people C. T. Studd wrote about so colourfully. They were no 'chocolate soldiers'.

> Mark time, Christian heroes,
> Never go to war;
> Stop and mind the babies
> Playing on the floor.
>
> Wash and dress and feed them
> Forty times a week.
> Till they're roly poly-
> Puddings so to speak
>
> Chorus:
> Round and round the nursery
> Let us ambulate
> Sugar and spice and all that's nice
> Must be on OUR slate.

In the Early Church during the period of the Roman Empire, there were groups of *paraboloni* ('risk-takers' or 'gamblers') who engaged in frontier-type ministries to prisoners, plague-victims and the like. By behaving like this, Epaphroditus filled the gap which the Philippian believers were unable to fill, through no fault of theirs.

QUESTIONS FOR DISCUSSION – 2:12-30

1. How do you explain the relationship between our work and God's work in our Christian living (see verses 12-13)?

2. Do 'fear and trembling' have a valid place in modern Christian living?

3. Can you devise any tactics which would minimise complaints and arguments amongst the children of God (see verse 14)?

4. What do you understand by the term 'the day of Christ' (verse 16)?

5. Set out the main points Paul makes in setting out the character and emotions of Epaphroditus.

6. How should Christians recognise and show appreciation for people who win the respect of their fellow-believers (see verses 29 and 30)?

6

CONFIDENCE IN CHRIST: PHASE ONE
BEWARE
3:1–6

Finally, my brothers, rejoice in the Lord! It is no trouble for me to write the same things to you again, and it is a safeguard for you. [2] Watch out for those dogs, those men who do evil, those mutilators of the flesh. [3] For it is we who are the circumcision, we who worship by the Spirit of God, who glory in Christ Jesus, and who put no confidence in the flesh – [4] though I myself have reasons for such confidence.

If anyone else thinks he has reasons to put confidence in the flesh, I have more: [5] circumcised on the eighth day, of the people of Israel, of the tribe of Benjamin, a Hebrew of Hebrews; in regard to the law, a Pharisee; as for zeal, persecuting the church; as for legalistic righteousness, faultless.

Beware of Dogs (3:1-3)

The discussion on verse 1 begins with the meaning of the words *to loipon* (NIV 'Finally') at the head of the chapter. Do they indicate a closing section, or a continuation? There are 44 more verses after this statement, and similarly in 1 Thessalonians there are 46 verses to follow this phrase. There is no way that such a lengthy and important section of the letter should be reckoned to be some kind of postscript or afterthought. Therefore, although *loipos* means ' (the) rest' or '(the) remainder' it should perhaps be regarded as a pick-up phrase, like 'very well then' (see 1 Thessalonians 4:1; 2 Thessalonians 3:1; 'still' in Mark 14:41; 'from now on' in 1 Corinthians 7:29; 'now' in 2 Timothy 4:8). Chapter Three brings us to a turning point. Paul has been going over some difficulties which would normally be thought of as likely to destroy, at least temporarily, their 'joie de vivre' as Christians. On the issue of his imprisonment, he is saying, 'Don't worry about me, for to me to live is Christ, and to die is gain. As far as false brethren are concerned, rejoice that Christ is preached, even if it is done from wrong motives. Minimise the effects of jealousy, envy and division by having the "Jesus Mind-set". Banish your sense of separation by recognising that God is at work in you. And don't fret about Epaphroditus' illness – I am sending him to you.'

In other words, to use a cinematic phrase, Paul is encouraging his Christian readers to return to the 'big picture' of rejoicing. (A visit to the cinema used to include two films, 'A' rated and 'B' rated respectively, the former being known as 'the big picture'). Rejoicing appears throughout the letter like the repeated theme in a symphony or overture (see 1:4, 18; 2:17, 18, 29; 3:1; 4:4, 10). The word **rejoice** is in the imperative mood, which indicates command mode. The joy of the Lord is never forced or artificial. It is not putting on a silly grin and pretending to be what you are not. The over-riding imperative for Christian servants to rejoice takes precedence over the following options, if I can paraphrase them, and is a kind of safeguard in the face of them:

1. Imitations – rejoice that Christ is preached, even out of wrong motives (1:15-18).
2. Imprisonment – don't worry about me; living is Christ, and dying is gain (1:21).
3. Jealousy/envy/division – maintain your joy and unity by having the Jesus mind-set (2:1-11).
4. Separation from those you love – God is at work in you, even when I am not with you (2:13).
5. Illness – God can give His presence, His healing, and His restoration. I am returning His servant, whose life God has spared, to you (2:25).

Therefore, in the first part of **verse 1**, Paul puts rejoicing as 'the big picture'. In the second part of verse 1, the apostle underlines the value of repetition of foundational truth for both teacher and hearers. At school I had two French teachers at different times in my school course. One of them was a douce and methodical lady whose life was totally organised around her teaching, and who was utterly shocked when pupils forgot anything she had taught them. She could probably have retrieved from her copious notebooks the date and time when she taught them any particular truth. The other was a rollicking man of the world, who believed that if he told you something a million times, you might remember it. I am sure the repetition of teaching material is one of the explanations for the occurrence of similar material in different times and places in the Gospels. Jesus repeated His teaching so that it would perhaps sink in. Paul belonged to the school of repetition in his teaching approach, and he found repetition of known truth was something which gave him sanity and his hearers security ('not irksome to me ... safe for you'). Christians are sometimes like the Athenians (Acts 17:21). They spend too much time 'talking about and listening to the latest ideas', and always lusting after something new. The best antidote against the bitter taste which robs us of our joy, is to remember and rejoice at God's gracious dealings with us in the past, and to do what Alexander Whyte of Edinburgh recommended, which was to 'roll them under your tongue like a sweetie!'

In **verse 2,** Paul gives the first episode of 'topsy-turvy teaching', on the theme of 'dogs' (see verse 3 for the second episode, i.e. regarding circumcision). This epithet was used sometimes, by Jews, of 'Gentile dogs', but here Paul switches it to apply to the Judaisers who were troubling the Philippian church. Then, as now, there were two kinds of dogs in the culture of the Middle East; pet dogs and pariah dogs. He is not thinking here of the pampered lap-dogs of the rich. He is thinking of the mangy scroungers of the back-streets, which you can meet in any city of the developing world. The comparison of their basic characteristics would apply to the Judaisers, in Paul's thinking. Like the pariah dogs, they are unpredictable in their reactions, indiscriminate in their tastes, and dangerous in their influence. There are stinging social and religious overtones in his use of the word 'dog', which was an insulting Old Testament term for a male cult prostitute (see Deut. 23:18; 1 Kgs 14:24; 15:12). The term is used in the category of those excluded from the heavenly city in Revelation 22:15. By using blunt language like 'dogs', Paul is following the straightforward line taken by the Lord Jesus Christ in Matthew 7:15: 'Watch out for false prophets. They come to you in sheep's clothing, but inwardly they are ferocious wolves.' Paul experienced them at close quarters, snapping at his heels.

At the start of **verse 2,** the believers are warned to 'look out' for them (see Mark 13:33, 'Take heed, watch'). 'Beware' (AV) doesn't fit the mood very well. This is Christianity with eyes wide open, alert to and aware of the threat of false teachers in the contemporary church, as well as the church of the New Testament period. Sometimes we are obliged, in view of impending danger, to pray with at least one eye open.

In **verse 3**, Paul continues his 'topsy-turvy teaching' by contending that Christians (both Jew and Gentile) are the true circumcision (see Jer. 4:4; Rom. 3:29; 9:24), rather than Jews (see Rom. 2:25-29; Eph. 2:11). The Temple curtain which symbolised Jew/Gentile division, has been torn down by God's initiative (heaven to earth/top to bottom), because of what Jesus has done (Matt. 27:51; Heb. 10:20). The Philippian letter gives glorious snapshot definitions of real worship and real Christianity. Here are three features of 'the real thing', from verse 3:

1. Spirit-led worship, which springs from desire, not duty, and is a choice, not a chore. Since the Holy Spirit is shed abroad in the hearts of God's people, their worship springs from an inner source, and is not like a superficial varnish. The desire to worship God wells up willingly in the hearts of His people.

2. Christ-centred joy, a characteristic of people who 'exult in Christ Jesus'. This distinctively Pauline verb (see 1:26) occurs about 35 times in his writings, and only twice elsewhere in the New Testament ('take pride' in James 1:9 and 'boast' in an evil sense in James 4:16). The Lord Jesus and His great work on the Cross are their boast as well as their basis. Sometimes Christians don't seem joyful. Martin

116

Luther was surprised one day when his wife Katy went upstairs and changed into black clothing. 'What's wrong, dear?' the great reformer asked her. She replied 'By the look of you, I thought that God had died an hour ago.'

3. Spiritual confidence, which repudiates any earthbound foundation (Gal. 6:14). 'The flesh' typifies human nature in its ignorance, weakness and error (Rom. 7:5). In 1 Corinthians 1:18 following, Paul sets out the message of the cross as a ground for boasting. Christians should reflect on their own lowly origins. Few of them had any 'clout' or influence in their social circle. But God had chosen them, and one of the foundational pillars of His choice was 'so that no one should boast before Him'. Now, the Philippian letter makes it clear – we have a new ground for boasting. It is Jesus we rejoice and exult in! He is the subject of the sentence of our lives. As Paul is about to point out, we dare not glory in upbringing, nationality, or training. We glory in him alone. We worship Him alone. This section challenges all of us as to whether our worship is the genuine article; a matter of heart and spirit, rather than the flesh.

Paul sums up his position beautifully and definitely in Galatians 6:14: 'May I never boast except in the cross of our Lord Jesus Christ, through whom the world has been crucified to me, and I to the world.' The Galatians text demonstrates not only that Paul's experience of the cross had altered his world-view, but also it had altered Paul. In the light of what Christ had done for him, he evaluated his world, including his past, differently. But Christ had also, in a sense, spoiled him for the world for good. Christians are able to share and identify with the apostle in this. Nothing that had pleased him in the past could ever please him again in the same way, because nothing could give him the same overwhelming sense of a mind at ease and a heart at peace with God that the experience of Christ's forgiveness had given him. That is why a backslidden Christian is the most miserable person on the face of God's earth. Paul had come to know God, and had continued in daily dependence on Christ, and this letter should encourage all of us to persevere in our Christian profession, and to glory in nothing and no-one else but Christ.

Many Jews gloried in the rite of circumcision. They exulted in their circumcision as a special sign of their being set apart for God. Circumcision was for the Jews a guarantee ticket to salvation. Although many of the nations of the Ancient Near East (e.g., Edomites, Moabites, and Arabs) practised circumcision, mainly for reasons of hygiene, for the Jew it was a special sign locked into the covenant made with Abraham (Gen. 17:9-14, 23-27; 21:4), and was a special sign of the spiritual separateness of the nation of Israel. The spiritual overtones of the Old Testament make it clear that in Israelite belief circumcision meant much more than the surgical removal of the foreskin. Jeremiah writes about an uncircumcised ear (Jer. 6:10) and an uncircumcised heart (Jer. 9:25-26), and in Exodus 6:12 and 30, Moses bemoans his uncircumcised lips. The general image seems to be that of fitness or competence to understand, feel or speak God's word, as well as being sexually prepared to join the nation. In later Judaism, the thought seems to have developed to include qualification to avoid Gehenna, the place of the damned. Rabbi Levi, around AD100, wrote: 'At the last, Abraham will sit at the entrance to Gehenna, and will not let any circumcised man of Israel go down there.' In the mercy of God, Paul had seen his great need of the Lord Jesus Christ in his life, and had made a complete U-turn, with humble faith replacing what was essentially proud complacency.

Beware of Display (3:4-6)

Self-Centredness (vv. 4-6)

In **verse 4**, Paul turns from 'we' to 'I'. If you ever find yourself passing a building site regularly, the wooden surrounds seem to be there for ages before the building gets under way. In this passage, Paul is like a sensible builder who spends a surprising amount of time clearing the site. Before he sets out his new foundation of confidence in Christ, he feels he has to show those aspects of his past self-confidence, which were built on the shaky foundations of his own in-born advantages and achievements built on effort. His life had been like the city of Jerusalem as Nehemiah described it on the return from Exile – 'there is ... much rubble' (Neh. 4:10). He sets out his own 'boasting stall' in a graphic way, which from a human angle would outdo any Judaising or Gentile claims of superiority, and consigns all of it to the scrap-heap (or, more accurately, the dung-heap), in comparison to the 'surpassing greatness of knowing Christ Jesus' (3:8).

Paul sets out his pre-conversion credentials in verses 5 and 6 by listing eight privileges which he could reckon as his. In the first part of **verse 5,** Paul lists what might be called the *advantages of heritage*:

The Rite of Circumcision. 'Circumcised the eighth day'. This was in strict agreement with God's procedures set out in the Torah (Gen. 17:12; Lev. 12:3). Isaac (Gen. 21:4) and Jesus (Luke 2:21) were circumcised on the eighth day. The Ishmaelites postponed circumcision until their boys were thirteen years old (Gen. 17:25). It was possible that some of the Judaising opponents of Paul addressed here were Gentile proselytes who were circumcised in adulthood. Therefore Paul's heritage had provided him with an innate advantage from day eight. Paul's ideas on the dignity of being born a Jew are expressed in Romans 3:1-2: 'What advantage, then is there in being born a Jew, or what value is there in circumcision? Much in every way....'

Racial Purity: 'Of the people of Israel.' His racial strain was altogether 'clean'. He was not of mixed origin, unlike the Ishmaelites who were also Abraham's descendants, and the Edomites who were the offspring of Abraham and Isaac – he was descended from Abraham, Isaac and Jacob. The last of these had received a name-change from 'the queue-jumper' (Jacob) to 'prince of God' (Israel).

Renowned Patriotism – 'Of the tribe of Benjamin.' The Benjamites had a chequered history in Israel, with some dark threads emerging from the pattern, like the Benjamite War, with its disgusting atrocities, and the Rape at Shiloh, during the period of the 'champions' (Judg. 19:22-26; 21:20, 21). Shimei, who cursed and threw stones at King David (2 Sam. 16:5-14), was a Benjamite, who finally got his just deserts (1 Kgs 2:36-46). Nevertheless, the tribe known as 'little Benjamin' had a special niche in Israelite history. Their progenitor was the only son of Israel born in the homeland of Canaan to Rachel, his favourite wife (Gen. 35:16-20). Israel's first king Saul was a Benjamite (1 Sam. 9:1, 2). Benjamin joined Judah to become the only tribes loyal to the dynasty of David at the Division of the Kingdom (1 Kgs 12:21). Like the Kerrs among the Scottish clans, the Benjamites were trained to fight left-handed, a distinct advantage in sword-fighting against right-handers. The Benjamites occupied an important position in time of battle (Judg. 5:14), providing slingers for the Israelite army (Judg. 20:16). In the story of Esther, the Jews' favourite Old Testament book, Mordecai, who encouraged Esther to go in to the king and intercede for the Jews, was a Benjamite.

Linguistic Purity: 'A Hebrew of Hebrews.' The term

'Hebrew' is as old as the descriptive phrase in Genesis 14:13 'Abram the Hebrew.' The term was probably used originally of a social class rather than an ethnic group, existing in Akkadian forms like 'Habiru/Hapiru/',Apiru/'Abiru' in the Early Bronze Age. The Habiru were a rootless, landless, melange of donkey caravaneers, mercenary warriors, highwaymen, and herdsmen. In the Bible, the term 'Hebrew' is generally applied to Israelites by outsiders, or by an Israelite speaking of himself to outsiders. The term evolved into an ethnic term, exclusively in the Old Testament, and eventually tapered by new Testament times into a linguistic definition of those Aramaic-speaking Jews who were not specifically influenced by Hellenism (Acts 6:1), or a term of contrast distinguishing them from Gentiles (2 Cor. 11:22). Acts 21:40 uses the term 'Hebrew' in relation to those who spoke Aramaic. The desire to retain racial and linguistic distinctives was heightened from the period of the Babylonian Exile onwards, and the Jews developed careful record-keeping in their family histories. The pure strain of Paul's parents had produced a pure strain in his linguistic abilities. The idiom used probably yields the meaning 'the Hebrew son of Hebrew-speaking parents'. Sometimes Jews in the homeland or of the Diaspora lost the cutting edge of their national faith and culture through absorption into the cultural and linguistic context where they lived. Nehemiah 13:23-27 outlines this sad situation, and Nehemiah's somewhat violent reaction to it: 'I rebuked them and called curses down on them. I beat some of the men and pulled out their hair'(!) Perhaps some of the Judaisers Paul opposed had a mere smattering of knowledge of written or spoken Hebrew. This was not so in Paul's case. He had been reared with this as the language of heart and hearth, not simply the language of learning in a synagogue or Temple context.

In the latter part of **verse 5** and into **verse 6** Paul lists the *advantages of effort*:

Commitment of Time: 'in regard to the law, a Pharisee.' Within Judaism, the Pharisees had started off as a kind of Jewish Scripture Union group. They would regard themselves as the custodians of the spirit and outlook of the Hasidim ('the Loyalists', derived from the Hebrew word *hesedh*) of the Maccabean period (mid-second century BC), who resisted the temptations to compromise posed by Greek culture (Hellenism) and the Seleucid kings, especially Antiocus IV Epiphanes. The Pharisees picked up the baton handed on from the non-political wing of the Hasidim, and became a powerful force during the period of the Hasmonean priest-king John Hyrcanus (135–104 BC). By the time of Josephus, they numbered over six thousand in Israel, and through their block vote held a controlling interest in the Jewish Council, the Sanhedrin. Their name probably means 'separatists', from the Hebrew word *parash* = 'to separate', They are described by Flavius Josephus (ca AD 66) as 'a body of Jews with a reputation of excelling the rest of their nation in the observance of religion, and as exact exponents of the laws'. The separatist dimension may relate to their separation from the 'people of the land' ('*am ha-arets*'), whose slack attitude to the Torah they regarded as impeding the Messiah's return.

The Pharisees were committed to total obedience not only to the Law, or Torah, revealed in the Pentateuch (Genesis to Deuteronomy), but to the corpus of scribal interpretation of the Torah. In the commandment department, for instance, Pharisaic tradition committed them to the other 603 commandments spun from the Decalogue by its interpreters. Lots of these commandments were rules of behaviour relating to the Sabbath. They had clearly defined Messianic hopes, a developed angelology, and firm belief in resurrection from the dead.

Because of their clearly defined membership and community rules, they were regarded as somewhat aloof from the hoi polloi, meeting in their fellowship groups for lunch and pre-Sabbath study times on Fridays. They would have regarded themselves as the custodians of the responsibility to justify the ways of God to men by life and lip. To some Jews their lives would seem salutary, and they would inspire respect and admiration.

Some Pharisees would live lives of scholarly and fastidious devotion, with gravity and dignity. Saul of Tarsus was probably one of those. However, an approach like this in Christianity or Judaism breeds elitism, and at its worst, the proud figure so deftly presented in Jesus' parable in Luke 18:9-14. 'Let him that thinketh he standeth take heed lest he fall!' A Boston preacher of the nineteenth century is supposed to have demonstrated that he missed the whole point of our Lord's parable, by closing a sermon based on the passage with a prayer, 'We thank Thee, Lord that we are not like this Pharisee'! Jesus obviously regarded their legal embroidery as an imposition on both the Law and the people who were called to keep it. He reserved some of His strongest words for them as ostentatious snobs (Matt. 6:2), poisonous snakes (Matt. 23:33), stupid hair-splitters (Matt. 23:16-22) and disgusting play-actors (Matt. 23:3, 13).

The Pharisees not only despised 'this rabble which cares nothing for the law' (John 7:49), but had ruled out Galilee as a seed-bed for prophets (John 7:52). Nazareth was a 'you've got to be kidding' kind of place too, with no defensive walls, so insignificant that it was not included in the list of Northern towns provided by Joshua and Josephus. Therefore Jesus as a teacher from 'where?' had no credence or standing with them. There is a veiled expression of doubt as to His parentage in John 8:41: '"we are not illegitimate children," they protested. "The only Father we have is God Himself.'" Jesus had not been to Jerusalem to study with any of the top Rabbis, like Gamaliel, whom Paul had studied with (Acts 22:3), in 'the strictest sect of our religion' (Acts 26:5). The brightest boys of the Diaspora synagogues were picked out and sent to engage in intensive study programmes with the top Rabbis in Jerusalem. Paul retained his loyalty to the law of God (Rom. 7:12, 14) and used his background as a Pharisee when he faced the Sanhedrin (Acts 23:6).

The Pharisees also resented the fact that, while they quoted the authorities, Jesus spoke with authority (Matt. 7:29). He seemed to contravene their food laws, and was quite unscrupulous in His contacts with people they regarded as unclean and outcast. The followers of such a local teacher would be perceived as part of a pernicious sect, to be snuffed out at all costs.

Commitment of Energy: 'as for zeal, persecuting the church'. Saul would regard it as a sacred commission from God to do everything in his power to rid the land of those who followed the hated Jesus of Nazareth. His driven nature is seen in his description of himself in Acts 26:5ff: 'They have known me for a long time and can testify, if they are willing, that according to the strictest sect of our religion, I lived as a Pharisee ... I too was convinced that I ought to do all that was possible to oppose the name of Jesus of Nazareth. And that is just what I did in Jerusalem. On the authority of the chief priests I put many of the saints in prison, and when they were put to death, I cast my vote against them. Many a time I went from one synagogue to another to have them punished, and I tried to force them to blaspheme. In my obsession against them, I even went to foreign cities to persecute them.'

Commitment of Heart: 'as for legalistic righteousness, faultless.' The main idea behind the Old Testament word for righteousness (*tsidheqah*) is that of conformity to a norm, or template or pattern. To illustrate, any reader might be looking for pear-shaped pears in a supermarket (a forlorn hope!). The pear shape is the norm for being a pear. The norm in matters of Pharisaic righteousness would be the character of God, and conformity to it, as set out in the revealed law, and the corpus of interpretation attached to it. The name 'Torah' itself comes from the Hebrew verb 'to shoot', so that Torah means 'direction' rather than 'law'. The 'Ten Words' or Ten Commandments relate initially and primarily to the character of God, and the desired human behavioural responses to Him. This would be the goal to which all their living would be directed.

Some of Paul's statements in Romans 7 indicate his desire to keep 'the five-fifths of the Law'. 'The Law is holy and the commandment is holy, righteous and good ... the law is spiritual ... I have the desire to do what is good ... in my inner being I delight in God's law' (verses 12, 14, 18, 22). At least as far as observable performance was concerned, Paul could claim to be 'faultless', *amemptos*, better 'blameless' (see 2:15, 'blameless and pure'). In this contest, could the performance of the Judaisers stand up in comparison to Paul's?

If the account of Paul's struggle for holiness in Romans 7 is a real account of his experience as a Christian after conversion, it reveals the superficiality of the Pharisaic outlook (see 1 Sam. 16:7). In Romans 7, Paul was painfully aware that he was anything but faultless. In fact, although his nationality, upbringing and training was radically different from most of us, the important and common factor is that each Christian has been gripped or 'taken hold of' (see verse 12) by the Lord Jesus Christ. The wonder of it is not removed because we do not share a 'Damascus Road' type of conversion experience. God is the God of infinite variety. To use the analogy of birth, some babies have a quiet, apparently uneventful entrance into the world. Other babies are born in crisis. Mother is rushed to hospital in the dead of night, and there is uproar and upset, and things seem unplanned and messy. The new birth is the same. One of my friends became a Christian at the age of five when he had a quiet talk with his mum, and a prayer was said by the fireside. Another young Christian friend claims his mother led him to Christ while washing his knees at the sink when he was three years old! John Newton became a Christian through a storm at sea. Some of our Christian friends cannot recall a specific time or event related to their being born again. It doesn't matter! James Philip uses an illustration relating the issue to appendicitis. Some people have a health crisis which necessitates the removal of their appendix, but we cannot make this the norm for having good health. For some people, the work of God in their lives is as quiet as the Lord opening Lydia's heart like a flower to His love. The important thing is to know that it has happened, and that your life is hidden with Christ in God, and that you have the same sense of belonging to the Lord Jesus Christ that Paul had.

QUESTIONS FOR DISCUSSION – 3:1-6

1. Are there any people around today's church who are equivalent to the 'dogs' Paul is writing about?

2. Discuss whether you think self-confidence a quality Christians should cultivate, in the light of verse 3 onwards? Set out possible modern grounds for it.

3. Is it ever wrong to be patriotic and nationalistic (please don't resort to physical violence in discussing this question!)?

4. Can you give examples of Christians who have given up a lot in order to serve Christ? Was it worth it?

5. Discuss the verdict that 'Christians are masochists' in the light of verse 10b: 'I want to know ... the fellowship of His sufferings, becoming like Him in His death.'

7

CONFIDENCE IN CHRIST: PHASE TWO
ASSESS/ANTICIPATE
3:7–21

[7] But whatever was to my profit I now consider loss for the sake of Christ. [8] What is more, I consider everything a loss compared to the surpassing greatness of knowing Christ Jesus my Lord, for whose sake I have lost all things. I consider them rubbish, that I may gain Christ [9] and be found in him, not having a righteousness of my own that comes from the law, but that which is through faith in Christ – the righteousness that comes from God and is by faith. [10] I want to know Christ and the power of his resurrection and the fellowship of sharing in his sufferings, becoming like him in his death, [11] and so, somehow, to attain to the resurrection from the dead.

[12] Not that I have already obtained all this, or have already been made perfect, but I press on to take hold of that for which Christ Jesus took hold of me. [13] Brothers, I do not consider myself yet to have taken hold of it. But one thing I do: Forgetting what is behind and straining towards what is ahead, [14] I press on towards the goal to win the prize for which God has called me heavenwards in Christ Jesus.

[15] All of us who are mature should take such a view of things. And if on some point you think differently, that too God will make clear to you. [16] Only let us live up to what we have already attained.

[17] Join with others in following my example, brothers, and take note of those who live according to the pattern we gave you. [18] For, as I have often told you before and now say again even with tears, many live as enemies of the cross of Christ. [19] Their destiny is destruction, their god is their stomach, and their glory is in their shame. Their mind is on earthly things. [20] But our citizenship is in heaven. And we eagerly await a Saviour from there, the Lord Jesus Christ, [21] who, by the power that enables him to bring everything under his control, will transform our lowly bodies so that they will be like his glorious body.

Christ-Centredness 3:7-14

In **verse 7** and the first part of **verse 8**, Paul gives a profit and loss inventory of his life. Anything he had gained from hereditary advantage or energetic achievement or moral uprightness he allows to pass before his mind, to calculate or rationally reckon (*egemai*) as moving from the Judaism 'gain' column of his life into the Christian 'loss' column. The Damascus Road experience (see Acts 9:1-19) had brought him such a blinding experience of the reality of the risen Christ and His forgiving grace, that everything else was, relatively, a dead loss. All his hours of book-learning paled into insignificance beside his new, personal knowledge of Christ living in his heart by faith, and the Spirit of Christ metamorphosing Paul, as the life of God sweetly conditioned the soul of this man, Paul the believer.

His friends would write him off as a waster, a disgrace to Judaism, a deranged deserter from the cause. Although his former family and communal life as a Jew had gone, and he no longer had the assured results of scholarship of the Torah, he was now a sinner saved by the sheer grace of God experiencing the surpassing joy of possessing Christ as his Saviour. The word translated 'loss' in verse 8 (*zemian*) is used of the precious cargo jettisoned from the ship in Acts 27:10, 21 and 38, so that the sailors and passengers would gain their lives. To revert to the 'topsy-turvy teaching' of verses 2 and 3, the world's advantages can become disadvantages in the 'winning-Christ' stakes. He piles on the epithets and adds a possessive pronoun when describing his Redeemer 'Christ Jesus my Lord'. Newton's hymn comes to mind:

Jesus my Shepherd, Saviour, Friend,
My Prophet, Priest and King.
My Lord, my Life, my Way, my End,
Accept the praise I bring.

131

To Paul, Jesus is like the treasure and the costly pearl Jesus Himself pictured in His parable. It is worth it to give up everything to have Him (Matt. 13:44-46; Ps. 73:25). John Sung, the great Chinese evangelist, got rid of all his books after a lengthy period of disciplined study, and became a man of one book (apart from his daily newspaper and his beloved photo album filled with photos of people he had led to Christ, and prayed for every day). Paul is now a man of one book and one Saviour, one passport to heaven and one consuming passion to spread the gospel. The residue of his past is 'rubbish' (**verse 8**). The Greek word is *skubala*, either a composite noun from *to tois kusi ballousin* = 'what is thrown to the dogs', or 'rubbish', 'dung' (used specifically, in the Sibylline Oracles, of human excrement). He wants the awareness of Christ to be so real and permanent that at any moment he can be 'found' (**verse 9**) almost inadvertently 'in Him' (see on 'in Christ' 1:1).

The element of surprise is there. Being in Christ, he is discovered in a new state, cut adrift now from legal performance, or human effort and achievement, as a basis for a right standing before God, but now lashed, like a sailor in a storm, to Christ whose qualities as Saviour mean that the empty hand of faith stretched out to Him is filled with a righteousness transferred out of His account. Hence 'a righteousness ... which is through faith in Christ' (verse 9). It is impossible to overdraw on this account – how can we exhaust the inexhaustible?!

The faith Paul is writing about is a God-given, confident trust in the total package of Christ's self-giving love (see Ephesians 2:8: 'For it is by grace you have been saved, through faith + and this not from yourselves, it is the gift of God'). Verse 9b echoes and underscores the Divine source and the faith channel by which our righteousness comes to us.

The whole question of how we can become right with God and righteous before God is at the heart of the Letter to the Romans. There Paul demonstrates how the world of the Gentiles, the Jews and the moralists had failed to attain to being right with God. The whole world was defiled and guilty, and culpable before Almighty God. God's way of putting people right with Him was through faith in Christ's death on the Cross (Rom. 3:25ff), which had become the focus of God's offering mercy to sinners, rather like the lid of the Ark of the Covenant on the Day of Atonement (see Leviticus 16). People become Christians by exercising faith in Christ as Saviour. This teaching on righteousness is basic and central. Verse 9 here deals with our justification, verse 10 with our sanctification and verse 11 with our glorification.

In **verse 10,** the apostle sets out the special desire of every believer – to engage in a growing awareness of the presence of Christ and the application of all His work to our lives. The verb 'to know' here is in the form of an articular infinitive of purpose (*to gnonai*), so that the NIV phrase 'I want' is supplied or deduced from the form of the verb rather than the words of the text. The purposive form of the verb flows naturally from the clauses of purpose in verse 8 ('that I may gain Christ') and verse 9 ('and be found in Him') and completes the sequence. The whole drift of verse 10 takes us away from relying on a display of human achievement to relying on an unfolding revelation of the Lord Jesus Christ, having a growing awareness of His presence, and a deepening appreciation of His love. First Peter 1:8 and 9 sum it up well: 'Though you have not seen Him, you love Him; and even though you do not see Him now, you believe in Him, and are filled with an inexpressible joy, for you are receiving the goal of your faith, the salvation of your souls.' Paul has become captivated by Christ, and wants to be increasingly engulfed in a partnership with a Saviour who has suffered and died and risen for him. He does not want to be side-tracked by anything else. James Fergusson says: 'It is hard for people not to rely on things other than Christ, to win heaven by them.' The faith at the heart of this section is also at the heart of all true knowledge. The best antidote for our sinful propensity for self-deception, is getting to know the Lord Jesus better.

In the words of verse 10, Paul wants to know:

1. *The person of his Lord*: 'I want to know Christ.' Christianity is Christ, and, at its base, Christian knowledge is spiritual and personal rather than cerebral. It is not a question of studying a book, or understanding a set of principles, but of knowing a Person, being absorbed by the Saviour. The communication of the gospel leads to observation of the teaching and saving acts of Jesus, and results in a strengthening desire to know Him better.

2. *The power of his life*: 'and the power of His resurrection.' Paul had come to experience Christ's resurrection power in raising him from the death-state of sin to the life of grace. The genitive 'of ... resurrection' may be either a genitive of apposition, defining the content of His resurrection, i.e. 'the power that His resurrection is', or a genitive of origin, tracing the source of His resurrection, i.e. 'the power emanating from His resurrection'. Christians are people of the resurrection, and every Lord's Day, or even every day, is a festival of the resurrection. The resurrection of the Lord Jesus has been transformed from a historical event to a life-changing experience of Him by each believer. The resurrection becomes again a *dunamis* in the daily experience of Christians (this is of course the origin of our English words 'dynamite' and 'dynamic').

3. *The passion of his love*: 'and the fellowship of sharing

in His sufferings.' It was P. T. Forsyth who said 'God is holy love'. The love of God is also a suffering love. In Romans 8:17, Paul writes that we 'share in His sufferings in order that we may also share in His glory'. In 2 Corinthians 1:7 and 8, the apostle writes: 'And our hope for you is firm, because we know that just as you share in our sufferings, so also you share in our comfort. We do not want you to be uninformed, brothers, about the hardships we suffered in the province of Asia. We were under great pressure, far beyond our ability to endure, so that we despaired even of life.' Of course, we can never fully enter into the experiences of suffering our Lord went through, as the Sinless One becoming the Sin-bearer, for example. H. R. Mackintosh makes out a case that the temptations of Christ were an exquisite form of torture because of His heightened sensitivity to sin, in comparison to us whose sensitivities have been damaged and blunted through our sinful practices.

Nevertheless, there is an individual and corporate sharing for each and every Christian in the awareness of the cost of our salvation, in the stigma of isolation and rejection which He must have felt, and which His people world-wide now feel, at the hands of detractors and rejectors. The writer remembers playing golf with a club member whose nickname was 'The Professor' (of English Language, they said, because of his foul tongue). After a miserable round when I had to suffer much blasphemy of the Lord's Name, he said 'I suppose my language upsets you.' My response was, 'Well, I try to put some of it down to lack of vocabulary, but since you asked me, I have to say that if you knew the Lord Jesus the way I know Him, you would not speak about Him like that.' During that game of golf, I felt the stigma of being a Christian.

4. *The partnership of his loss*: 'becoming like Him in His death.' The translated phrase 'becoming like' is

summorphizomenos, which has at its core the word *morphe* meaning 'shape' or 'pattern'. The idea is of conformity, 'sharing the shape'. Galatians 2:20 teaches that we are 'crucified with Christ'. Dying to self is at the heart of the gospel, and the physical expressions of martyrdom seen at periods of persecution under Roman Emperors like Nero, Domitian and Diocletian involved an identification and incorporation into the pattern of suffering that Christ went through:

> It is the way the Master trod,
> Shall not the servant tread it still?

There may be uncertainty expressed in verse 11 ('somehow') about the route to the resurrection of the dead to which Christians look forward (1 Corinthians 15:22: 'For as in Adam all die, so in Christ all shall be made alive', and verse 52: 'for the trumpet will sound, and the dead shall be raised incorruptible, and we shall be changed'). This in no sense undermines the certainty of the destination. We shall reach the terminus!

In **verses 12-14,** Paul indicates another dimension in his repudiation of the 'display' of self-achievement. He has not 'arrived'. He has far to go. The logical progress of the thought takes us from knowing Jesus in verse 10 to following Him in verse 11. His imperfect performance as a Christian is a spur rather than a barrier to progress. He is ready to 'press on', like an athlete in a foot-race. In the early years of his missionary career in Africa, David Livingstone expressed his willingness for service to the London Missionary Society by saying he was 'willing to go in any direction, provided it was forward'.

Paul here has the right mental attitude of a heart and mind at ease with Christ's peace, coupled with a realistic appraisal of incompletion and imperfection. Paul borrows the familiar imagery of the first century world, where the spread of Greek culture encouraged the cult of the body, in stadium and gymnasium. He is like a man at the starting-blocks (or first century starting-stones), stripped to the bare essentials (see Hebrews 12:1), ready for action. In his experience of Christ he has been gripped by Christ, and is now given to Christ for the rest of his life. The motto of Spurgeon's College in London, England, is *Teneo et Teneor* = 'I hold and I am held'. Paul has not yet been made perfect, in the sense of a full, experiential sense of fulfilment in his Christian life. Most Christians are aware of the good hand of God on their life. One of my friends signs his letters to me, 'Yours in His Grip'. Sometimes it seems that we lose our grip on Him. There are many things that attempt to side-track us in Christian service, some of them attractive and legitimate. Being a Christian is a serious business, and by God's strength we can resist these blandishments. We can all echo the thought of Robert Frost in relation to the things that can be so alluring:

The woods are lovely, and very deep,
But I have many promises to keep,
And many miles to go before I sleep.

Part of the mental attitude of the athlete is a focussed concentration which blocks out recent activity ('forgetting what is behind', **verse 13**), and is fixed on immediate goals ('straining towards what is ahead', verse 13). The whole sweep of Paul's imagery of Christian activity here is expressed in the terse phrase 'one thing' (*hen de*). The verb 'I do' in the NIV has to be supplied to help the sense; it is not in the text. The entire Christian race is reviewed in the language of pursuing and overtaking, and laying hold on. The 'prize' (**verse 14**) he has in mind is probably Christ Himself (see verse 8 on 'gaining Christ'), and there is a vertical as well as a horizontal dimension included in the race ('heavenwards', verse 14).

Paul's goal and reward are retained in his positive thinking, even in the limiting circumstances of imprisonment. He looks back to his commissioning on the Damascus Road, and to the 'high calling of God in Christ Jesus' (Authorised Version translation of verse 14). (See, for example, 2 Timothy 1:8, 9 'God, who has saved us and called us to a holy life.') Athletes are encouraged to have a visual focus ahead of them. Since the imagery of running the Christian race is more aptly compared to a marathon rather than a sprint, we can note the direction given to marathon runners encountering 'the wall' at around the twenty-mile mark to look steadily at a point about six feet ahead of them. The hymn-writer Mary D. James says:

Since my eyes were fixed on Jesus,
I've lost sight of all beside;
So enchained my spirit's vision,
Gazing at the Crucified.

In the matter of our sanctification, Christians should be committed to hopes of change and progress. We should not be swilling about in the same old sins, like pigs in the trough. Murray McCheyne's prayer should be ours: 'Lord, make me as holy as it is possible for a pardoned sinner to be.' In this mode, we are delivered from the rat-race for display which is such an ugly thing in some Christian lives.

Beware of Dissention (3:15-21)

The devil loves nothing better than division within the church of Jesus Christ. Two of the worst things a church can do is to appoint unspiritual people to positions of spiritual leadership in the church because of their wealth, cleverness or influence, and to promote a 'novice' to eldership functions (see 1 Timothy 3). In this section, especially in **verses 16 and 17**, Paul is warning against the dangers of a 'takeover' by those who are driven by appetite, physical or spiritual.

The NIV 'mature' in **verse 15** is a good rendering of *teleioi*, which is a favourite word of Paul, used to indicate the following:

1. The perfection of God's will (Rom. 12:2).
2. The physique of adulthood (Eph. 4:13; Col. 4:12) contrasted with infancy (1 Cor. 3:1).
3. The final contrasted with the partial (1 Cor. 13:9).
4. The fullness of an adult mind, contrasted with a child's mind (1 Cor. 14:20).

Some scholars think that the use of *teleioi* extends the 'topsy-turvy' teaching of Paul in verses 2 and 3 in providing a contrast with the Judaisers and their perfectionist tendencies. He is therefore presenting Christian believers as the genuine *teleioi*.

It is impossible to achieve God's righteousness goals in our lives by wearing the strait-jacket of law-keeping. The heavenward calling of the Lord Jesus brings us into a mature assessment of our position in Christ. In Romans 12:3, Paul writes : 'Do not be conceited, or think too highly of yourself; but think your way to a sober estimate, based on the measure of faith God has dealt to each of you' (New English Bible). We should therefore, he argues, be open to the Lord's leading if we find our spiritual attitude leads us into a different mind-set. In verse 16, he argues for our spiritual progress to be under the control of this constant regulator. This will be a preventative measure so that we do not slip back. The gospel is so sensible and practical!

Verses 17-21 expose the contrast between those who live and teach falsehood, and those who follow the pattern set out by the apostle. Scholarly opinion is divided as to whether Paul is characterising Judaisers or sensualists in verses 18-19. Those who identify them as Judaisers have to take a specific line in linking 'their god is their stomach' to Jewish food laws. Also, they argue, shouldn't Jewish rather than pagan behaviour be shocking enough to move him to tears? Perhaps the 'sensualists', with their greed and immorality, fit the text better. There aren't many Christians who can say 'follow my example, brothers', by displaying the Christian family likeness. He calls them to be *summimetai* ('fellow-imitators'). The 'sum-' part of the word probably intensifies the meaning that Paul has in mind for them, that this is community modelling of the Christian character of unselfishness, humility and service. Philippians 2:5-11 had set out the Christian mind-set in relation to Christ. Paul would mean of course that Christians should follow him as far as he followed Christ (see 1 Corinthians 11:1). The 'pattern' (verse 17) is *tupos* (translated 'example' in Titus 2:7, and 'copy' in Hebrews 8:5) is clearly visible to any with eyes to see, because Paul's tent-making ministry brought him into vital daily contact with people in their everyday lives, wherever he travelled (see 1 Thessalonians 1:5-7: 'You know how we lived among you for your sake. You became imitators of us and of the Lord ... and so you became a model to all the believers in Macedonia and Achaia'). It is better to follow the example of holy people (1 Cor. 11:1) than to be involved in the personality cult (1 Cor. 1:12).

By way of contrast, Paul tearfully delineates the character of the sensualists who are 'the enemies of the cross' (**verse 18**). Note again in passing that Paul is a man of strong emotions. The joy of the Lord is his strength, but to love deeply and feel deeply makes him vulnerable to hurtful words and actions, especially where the cause of Christ's church is concerned. He is no mere automaton performing a task to fulfil a programme, but a real man, affected by the behaviour of others around him. The 'pressure of my concern for all the churches' was something he faced daily (2 Cor. 11:28). At times he was like a nursing mother to the believers (see 1 Thess. 2:7), tenderly adapting to their present condition like a mother adapts her shape to that of her baby, communicating warmth and nourishment.

These enemies of the cross are heading for destruction (**verse 19**), an eternity of separation from God in the realm of outer darkness (Matt. 25:26-30). The Scottish motto *nemo me impune lacessit* ('no-one assails me with impunity') usurps the role of God the Judge who is the only One who has the ultimate power to punish and the prerogative of offering mercy. Their god and king is appetite ('whose god is their stomach', or beastly belly-god), their basis for boasting was the very thing they should be ashamed about (how many of us have heard sickening accounts of sexual conquests in staff-room, office, and locker-room?). They are earth-bound, like the man with the muck-rake in Bunyan's *Pilgrim's Progress*, who never looked up, or like the man described by Alexander Maclaren who kept heaping up the dust of the condemned cell, and calling it gold. The life-style described here perverts the mind as well as body and soul. The old Puritan writer James Fergusson says that 'the Lord sometimes suffers seducers to multiply in a church to punish the small respect given to truth'.

Verse 20 spells out where Christians belong. Their 'citizenship' (*politeuma*) is in heaven. This term embraces the Old Testament idea of the resident alien, or 'ger' (see, for example, Exodus 18:3: "One son was named Gershom, for Moses said, 'I am an alien, 'ger', in a foreign land.'"). It also reflects the fourth-century BC strategy of 'polis planting' which was a key feature of Alexander the Great's way of 'winning the peace' as well as the war. 'Politeuma' is related to the city (*polis*). Alexander settled wounded soldiers and veterans in the cities he had conquered, encouraging them to infiltrate and overcome the culture where they lived, spreading the pattern of Greek culture and city life as part of his plans to Hellenise the world. The term also reflects the organisation of the Roman Empire. The Romans, always expert plagiarisers, adopted the ideas of Hellenism and developed the 'colony' idea within the Empire. Philippi was a Roman colony, with *Ius Italicum* ('Italian privilege'), treated like a piece of territory transplanted from Italy (see Introduction, section 2).

In spiritual terms, God's grace makes Christians approach life from a heavenly perspective. Their names are 'written in heaven' (Luke 10:20), in the 'book of life' (Rev. 20:12, 15). Their outlook and behaviour are no longer conditioned by appetite and selfishness. It is not that they have been taken over by a forceful or quiet alien invasion, described, for example, in films like the fifties production *The Invasion of the Body Snatchers*. This is, after all, God's world, and He is in a sense taking what is His by right, and doing a work of resurrection and restoration, for we are made 'in His image, in His likeness' (Gen. 1:26).

The idea of being unworldly and godly, and the way of thinking that our home is really in heaven, has taken two kinds of hard knocks in recent years. On the one hand, people have used this concept as an excuse for opting out of society, refusing to vote in elections, take part in politics or local affairs, serve in armies, and so on. There have been extreme examples of the kind of people who do not go to public worship because they cannot find a church that is spiritual enough to suit their 'heavenly view' of things. They do not consider that were they to find the perfect church, it would immediately become imperfect were they to be welcomed into membership! The refusal to fulfil our civic obligations meets its corrective in the classic definition given by the Lord Jesus in Mark 12:17: 'Give to Caesar what is Caesar's and to God what is God's.' On the other hand, some Christians (not only young ones!) limbo-dance like mad to accommodate to the low standards imposed by a world which loves to 'squeeze you into its mould,' as J. B. Phillips puts it in translating Romans 12:2. The result is a pathetic, anaemic brand of Christianity which has lost all its distinctives. We should remember Joseph and Daniel, and launch a robust attack on the pernicious idea that to be heavenly-minded means necessarily to be of no earthly use. Godly people who set their mind and heart on things above (see Colossians 3:1-2) are a positive asset to the society in which they live. There they function as salt and light, part of God's providential restraint in the cut-throat rat-race of modern life.

Our heavenly citizenship gives us great expectations! We expect a 'Saviour' (*soter*), **verse 20**, to come again. The word *soter*, referring to Christ, is used by Paul only here in Ephesians 5:23: 'Christ is the Head of the church. His body, of which He is the Saviour', apart from its regular use in the Pastoral Letters (for example in 2 Timothy 1:10, and in the brilliant combination-phrase of Titus 2:13: 'our great God and Saviour, Jesus Christ'). Some scholars think the reason for the sparing use of the term is because it was an overworked word in pagan religion. Although the Lord Jesus Christ is the Judge of all men, Christians are eagerly expecting Him as Saviour. The absence of the definite article may be deliberate in the Greek text, to indicate a generic, representative function. Christians are 'being saved', in transit in the salvation process, and Jesus' coming will accelerate the process towards the consummation of God's Master-plan. The letter has anticipated this in earlier references, for example in 1:6, 21 and 23.

The Christian range of expectations includes our bodies. In pagan thought, the body was regarded as the clay prison-house of the soul. One school of thought tried to knock it into shape, like a disobedient slave. Another school of thought was that we could indulge our body's appetites to the full because there was no connection between the physical and the spiritual. In Christian teaching, our treatment of our bodies is a special stewardship from God. There is nothing intrinsically evil about our bodies. They can be abused and misused because of our nature as sinners. But they are part of the image of God in terms of our expression of worship, and they are, under the New Covenant, temples in which the Holy Spirit lives (1 Cor. 3:16, 17; 6:19). Because of the package included in the Fall, they are prone to ageing, decay, disease and death. Our physical and mental powers deteriorate. We go to a Sunday School picnic, and attempt to do with a ball what we used to do, and the result is ludicrous! Yet here we are in our earthly bodies, on our way to heaven. What is God going to do about that?

We expect the Lord Jesus Christ, our 'great God and Saviour' (Titus 2:13) to 'transform our lowly bodies' (**verse 21**). In the light of the teaching outlined above, the Authorised Version translation 'vile bodies' is clearly misleading. The word *tapeinoseos* is better rendered as in the NIV's 'lowly', and is nearer the normal sense of 'of low position, undistinguished'. Here comes the transforming Saviour! He has been transforming things since we first knew Him (2 Cor. 5:17). At our conversion, when we were born again, He transformed our spirits, giving them new life. Now it is the turn of our lowly bodies. He will 'transform' (*metaschematisei*') them. At the heart of this word is our English word 'scheme'. They are to be refashioned, refurbished, or renovated, transferred into a new scheme of things so that the outward appearance matches the inner form of a nature renewed by God's grace and Christ's power, and equipped for praise for all eternity. The form will now be that of the risen, ascended Lord Jesus Christ. 'When He appears, we shall be like Him, for we shall see Him as He is' (1 John 3:2). 'We shall be conformed to the image of His (God's) dear Son' (Rom. 8:29).

The mechanics of the change our Saviour, the Lord Jesus Christ, will accomplish derives its driving force from 1 Corinthians 15. Christ's resurrection is the basis on which we can hope for physical transformation (1 Cor. 15:20-22, 42-44). In the case of the Lord Jesus Christ, His resurrection body was sometimes recognisable, and had unusual powers. It is difficult, and perhaps unprofitable, to speculate as to what the Saviour is going to do for us.

We do know Christ's power (*dunamis*, verse 21) will be unleashed to accomplish this. The power exercised in action (*energeian*) will transmute our lowly bodies to be like (*summorphon*) His glorious (literally 'body of glory') body. The steps and stages of the process are outlined in Romans 8:29-30: 'For those God foreknew He also predestined to be conformed to the likeness of His Son ... and those He predestined, He also called; those He called He also justified; those He justified, He also glorified.' Young people starting off on the first rung of the ladder in business sometimes ask, 'Has the job any prospects?' Christians have great expectations and great prospects!

In relation to dissension, it is a good strategy to be positive, as Paul is here, and focus believers' attention on the Lord Jesus Christ as the centre of their thinking and their hopes. This also diverts their attention from the damaging and corrosive influences of those whom he calls 'the enemies of the cross'.

QUESTIONS FOR DISCUSSION – 3:7-21

1. Discuss the Bible teaching on forgetting. Does God forget? If so, what does He forget? What should we forget?

2. Can you think of other Bible teaching on the theme 'the Christian athlete' (see verses 13 and 14)? Could you highlight the main lessons on this theme?

3. See verse 16, and discuss the following ethical summary: 'Being a Christian is not so much being what you are not, as becoming what you are.'

4. Is it right to imitate other Christians (see verse 17 following)? Is it of limited value to us to do so?

5. Who are the 'enemies of the cross' (see verse 19) today?

6. Discuss the meaning of the phrases 'our lowly bodies' and 'His glorious body' (verse 21).

8

CONTENTMENT IN CHRIST
4:1–23

Therefore, my brothers, you whom I love and long for, my joy and crown, that is how you should stand firm in the Lord, dear friends!

[2] I plead with Euodia and I plead with Syntyche to agree with each other in the Lord. [3] Yes, and I ask you, loyal yokefellow, help these women who have contended at my side in the cause of the gospel, along with Clement and the rest of my fellow-workers, whose names are in the book of life.

[4]Rejoice in the Lord always. I will say it again: Rejoice! [5]Let your gentleness be evident to all. The Lord is near. [6]Do not be anxious about anything, but in everything, by prayer and petition, with thanksgiving, present your requests to God. [7]And the peace of God, which transcends all understanding, will guard your hearts and your minds in Christ Jesus.

[8] Finally, brothers, whatever is true, whatever is noble, whatever is right, whatever is pure, whatever is lovely, whatever is admirable – if anything is excellent or praiseworthy – think about such things.

[9] Whatever you have learned or received or heard from me, or seen in me – put it into practice. And the God of peace will be with you.

[10] I rejoice greatly in the Lord that at last you have renewed your concern for me. Indeed, you have been concerned, but you had no opportunity to show it. [11] I am not saying this because I am in need, for I have learned to be

content whatever the circumstances. ¹² I know what it is to be in need, and I know what it is to have plenty. I have learned the secret of being content in any and every situation, whether well-fed or hungry, whether living in plenty or in want. ¹³I can do everything through him who gives me strength.

¹⁴ Yet it was good of you to share in my troubles. ¹⁵Moreover, as you Philippians know, in the early days of your acquaintance with the gospel, when I set out from Macedonia, not one church shared with me in the matter of giving and receiving, except you only; ¹⁶ for even when I was in Thessalonica, you sent me aid again and again when I was in need. ¹⁷ Not that I am looking for a gift, but I am looking for what may be credited to your account. ¹⁸ I have received full payment and even more; I am amply supplied, now that I have received from Epaphroditus the gifts you sent. They are a fragrant offering, an acceptable sacrifice, pleasing to God. ¹⁹ And my God will met all your needs according to His glorious riches in Christ Jesus.

²⁰ To our God and Father be glory for ever and ever. Amen.

²¹Greet all the saints in Christ Jesus. The brothers who are with me send greetings. ²²All the saints send you greetings, especially those who belong to Caesar's household.

²³ The grace of the Lord Jesus Christ be with your spirit. Amen.

Sharing with Others (4:1-3)

In this passage, Paul emphasises to the Philippian brothers and sisters that as far as he is concerned they are loved and longed for. The thought of them makes his heart well up with joy as they display the Christian fruitfulness which caps all that he has worked for as a Christian leader. The fruit of the gospel is clearly seen in their actions. It is rather like a family situation, where you can have the joy of seeing the values you have inculcated into your children emerging in their childhood and adult behaviour patterns. I remember leading a Scripture Union camp (75 boys under canvas at Scoughall, near North Berwick) and observing one of my campers for ten days. He was brought late to camp by older-than-average parents. He was an unusual phenomenon – a godly boy, who joined in all the activities of the camp programme. He was quiet, showing a mature awareness of his fellow-campers, was respectful towards the leaders, and had a tremendous grasp of biblical truth in group discussion and the quizzes in the evening meetings. At the end of camp, he came to give me the remains of the pocket money his parents had given him for camp, for the 'God and Others' box. He had been given £10, a fraction of what others had, and had spent only £3.50 on himself at the camp tuck-shop. I thought that he was a tremendous credit to his parents, and it must have brought them great joy to have him at home. The Philippian church brought great joy to Paul as he watched them developing. They were his 'joy and crown' (verse 1). In the face of all the difficulties that would face them internally and externally, he calls them to dig in their heels and stay with gospel teaching.

Paul's tenderness is not in question here, and it is not simply a sugar coating for the bitter pill of 'church discipline' he is about to administer. In verse 2 he names two individuals – Euodia ('good journey') and Syntyche (possibly 'Lucky Lady' from 'sun' = 'with', or 'companion of'' Tyche, the goddess of fortune – see Acts 20:4,9, where we encounter Tychicus and Eutychus). Renderings of the names of this gruesome twosome have ranged from A. M. Hunter's 'Freedom and Felicity' to 'Odious and Soon-Touchy'! They were members, and possibly leaders (from Lightfoot onwards some reckon they are deaconesses, like Phoebe in Romans 16:1) in the Philippian church. Verse 3 makes it clear that they had been Paul's partners in the work, but they had lost their evangelical focus, and some unspecified disagreement had arisen between them. It is futile to speculate what this might have been. In the writer's experience, Christians are capable of disagreeing about anything, from whether a person with a bunion should be allowed to wear slippers to attend church, to whether a church kitchen cooker should have four or six rings! In any case, Paul calls them to agree in the Lord. The repetition of the word 'plead' in the NIV is true to the text, and indicates, literally, he is calling each of them alongside him for this purpose.

The appeal invites 'loyal yoke-fellow' (**verse 3**), which in some texts is transliterated as a proper name, Syzygos, to live up to his name ('joiner-together') and strengthen the partnership. Since in certain non-Biblical references, the term means 'wife', some scholars have thought that this is a reference to Paul's wife. This type of work, functioning as a go-between in a quarrel, is very energy-sapping in church life, and a lot of the energy used tends to be negative energy, which is not helpful in the cause of the gospel.

Paul is painstakingly striving to encourage group effort here, for he uses four words which are compounded with the preposition *sun* ('together'), compounded with nouns or verbs to strengthen its meaning, in **verses 2 and 3**. In Galatians 6:1, Paul highlights the specialist aspects of the work of restoration and reconciliation. He mentions it in the Galatians text as the work of 'you who are spiritual', (*hoi pneuamtikoi*) and he uses the verb *katartizo* a word of specialism, used in the Gospels of the fishermen disciples mending or overhauling their nets ('preparing' NIV), and in non-Biblical texts of a surgeon re-setting a dislocated limb. To borrow the latter metaphor, and to combine the two ideas, when people are out of fellowship, in disagreement, it is like having a dislocated limb in your body. It has a jarring effect on the whole body, and it is impossible to function harmoniously. Everyone is affected. Therefore, there are both general and special aspects of the work of restoration. Group prayer and loving interest are part of the general picture, but there is a place for specific action to heal the rift.

There are still lots of vacancies for people who will 'contend' for the gospel **(verse 3)**, be sound in its fundamentals, and defend it against its opponents. With regard to 'the book of life', the notion of divine record-keeping is at least as old as Malachi 3:16: 'Then those who feared the LORD talked with each other, and the LORD listened and heard. A scroll of remembrance was written in his presence concerning those who feared the LORD and honoured his name.' The 'book' is also featured in Daniel 12:1: The 'book of life' here needn't refer to dead saints, because the Lord Jesus told His disciples in Luke 10:20 that their 'names are written in heaven', which was far superior to having their names on the civic register of Philippi. The concept of a 'book of life' is prevalent in the Book of Revelation (3:5; 17:8; 20:12).

Controlling Yourself (4:4-9)

In these verses, Paul is highlighting, possibly in contrast with the behaviour of Euodia and Syntyche, positive features which will enhance good attitudes and behaviour. Ben Hogan, the champion golfer, compared the golf swing with the cowboy movies: 'If you set it up in favour of the good guys, the bad guys can't take over!' As with the golf swing, so with life!

In verses 4-9, the 'good guys' are:

Joy and gentleness (vv. 4 and 5).

A positive and active prayer life (vv. 6 and 7).

Highest-level thinking and good practice (vv. 8 and 9).

With **verse 4,** we are back to 'the big picture' (see comment on 3:1) of **rejoicing**. Consistent joy is a telling witness for the Lord.

In **verse 5**, he encourages a full display of **gentleness** (*epieikes*, a word compounded from *epi* ['upon'] as an intensifying preposition, and *eikos* ['reasonable']). See 2 Corinthians 10:1, where Paul bases his appeal on 'the meekness and gentleness of Christ.' See 1 Timothy 3:3 and Titus 3:2 where this quality is part of the 'identi-kit' of Christian leaders. The Authorised Version uses the word 'moderation', which conveys the idea of someone who is under control. When I was a milk delivery boy, the old Trojan vehicle the driver had was fitted with a 'governor' under the accelerator, which meant that no driver could suddenly make the engine roar into life. Perhaps it is the sign of advancing years, but there seem to be large numbers of inflammatory characters around nowadays. They operate as if there were no 'governor' operating in their lives, and flare up like fireworks: 'light touch paper and retire immediately!' Yet it is not fair to think of this quality the apostle mentions as merely passive or even negative. This God-given quality should act as our governor in our emotional extremes. A. T. Robertson says it is 'not negative restraint, but a positive giving up to the reasonable desires of others ... that leads one to go beyond the letter of the law, the stronger giving up to the weaker. The range of meaning covers fairness, decency, reasonableness, open-heartedness, and leniency, even in the face of injustice, hatred and malice, carried through with an unwavering trust in God, who is always present, as Paul reminds us here' (verse 5b, 'the Lord is at hand'). The Lord Jesus had taught this, of course, in the Sermon on the Mount (Matthew 5:7: 'Blessed are the merciful, for they will be shown mercy').

In **verses 6 and 7**, our Lord's teaching about **anxiety** is echoed in Paul. Worry and anxiety use up negative energy and rob us of peace and sleep. Paul's panacea, the positive antidote for worry, is **prayer**, and Paul moves from the 'anything' to the 'everything' of life, covering it all with a blanket of prayer in its three layers of 'prayer' (*proseuche*), in general request, 'petition' (*deesei*, which means specific mention of particular needs; the word implies a humble self-abasement); and thirdly, 'thanksgiving' (*eucharistias*), a healthy component which leads to praise, and contentment. We sometimes say 'prayer changes things', and sometimes 'prayer changes people', and in forming conclusions about this, the people most likely to be changed through prayer are ourselves. Prayer gives us such a perspective about God, and ourselves, that circumstances no longer seem to be of paramount importance.

In **verse 7b**, the apostle paints a picture in words of Peace the Warrior. It is noteworthy that the two word-pictures of peace in the New Testament are both very positive authority figures. Here, Paul recalls the figure of the Roman soldier on guard duty, a familiar sight throughout the Mediterranean world, where Rome was the occupying power. He pictures

Peace as a strong warrior, keeping our hearts and lives under control (see comment on 1:2). The Roman soldier on guard duty was expected to patrol the ramparts or city walls, repel unwelcome invaders and by his very presence keep the peace. God's peaceful control operates in the emotional 'hearts' and rational 'minds' areas of life for those who are 'in Christ Jesus'. A television producer was fielding complaints from an audience about the lateness of the hour for the 'God-slot' on television. He said that it did not matter how late they broadcast, there was always a substantial audience, because we (the British) have become a nation of insomniacs. People just cannot sleep because of worry and stress and unease of various kinds. One of the ways in which God moderates His peace to our hearts and minds is through sleep. Christians should always submit their sleep to the sovereignty of the Holy Spirit, who can mediate God's peace to us, even through our subconscious thought, while we are asleep. We sleep also with the certainty that the God who watches over us will 'neither slumber nor sleep' (Ps. 121:3-4).

The other picture of Peace in Paul's letters is that of an Umpire (Colossians 3:15: 'let the peace of Christ rule, or referee), another very positive image. The umpire moderates on the action of a game, enabling it to flow smoothly.

Verses 8 and 9 take us into the specifics of Christian thought, modelled in people like Paul. The Stoics had four virtues on their list. Paul lists six virtues here for the Christians, each covered by a 'whatever', with two 'ifs' added for good measure! The Lord's joy, brotherly unity, and a prayer life lead to a heart at peace and a mind at ease. The Christian life is an integrated life. It is like a home tastefully and carefully furnished, where the carpets are enhanced by the curtains, and so on. As these six 'whatever' qualities listed in verse 6 percolate through our minds, 'the peace of God' mentioned in verse 7 is intensified by the living presence of the 'God of peace' mentioned in verse 9. The passage reminds us musically of the recapitulation of familiar themes near the end of a symphony.

'Whatever is true' in **verse 8** relates to the 'truth' in verse 9 and is like a 'belt buckled round our waist' in the gospel armour of Ephesians 6:14. The 'noble' (*semna*) things of verse 8 are derived from the verb 'to worship or revere', and convey dignity, respect, and serious-mindedness in our Christian character and testimony. The link-word *semnotes* is the quality with which elders must run their homes (1 Tim. 3:4) and it should also be a character feature of aged men, deacons and their wives (1 Tim. 3:8-11; Titus 2:7). In the writings of the Early Church Fathers, it denotes quiet patience, a contrast with ill temper. This is all in contrast to the largely superficial and frivolous culture around us as we enter our garish, chromium-plated millenium. A people who have been made righteous should have 'whatever is right' (verse 8) as a bench-mark for all their living, so that they are fair and square in all their dealings. In his early business life, J. C. Penney went out of business as a butcher in Longmont, Colorado, rather than give a bottle of bourbon to a hotel chef every week as a 'sweetener'. God honoured Penney, and he master-minded a billion-dollar business empire, with over 1,400 stores nationwide, founded on Christian values.

In an atmosphere polluted with pagan impurity (Phil. 3:18-19), especially in the area of sexual impurity (pederasty and incest were rife), Christian minds should be as 'pure' (verse 8) as an unspoilt virgin. This is also true in the modern world. It is a better achievement to bring up children in a home centred on holiness than to write a sleazy best-seller filled with filth. The *lovely* things in verse 8 (*prosphilia*, here only in the New Testament) cover whatever is pleasing and agreeable. The **admirable** things (*euphema*, again here only in the New Testament) would relate primarily to speech, although it can have a musical connotation, like the pitch-perfect resonance of a well-tuned piano. Paul gathers up all these qualities in the comprehensive phrase *excellent or praiseworthy*. We should ask God to fill our minds with these good qualities so that there isn't any room for anything else. Meditation always has as valid a role in Christian experience as in any other world religion or New Age philosophy. The fundamental difference is that our Christian thought arises from our trust in a Person, it is Christ-focussed originally, and all our other thinking and living flows from that source. It isn't simply a matter of 'thinking beautiful thoughts' about God or nature.

As if to underline the personal aspects of Christian truth, in **verse 9**, in a breathtaking way for a humble Christian leader ('less than the least of all God's people', Ephesians 3:8), Paul moves from the realm of theological truth to incarnational truth. Our Christian learning curve has four phases, according to verse 9: **whatever you have learned, or received, or heard from me, or seen in me**. The believers have to put into practice the truths that Paul has embodied as well as taught (Phil. 3:17). We have to live in such a way that the things we say are not drowned out by the lives we live. To put it in other words, the Christian qualities inter-meshed in our lives have to provide confirmatory evidence of the reality of the gospel we preach. R. G. LeTourneau, inventor of the prototypes of nearly every piece of earth-moving equipment in use today, said: 'If you're not serving the Lord, it proves you don't love him. If you don't love Him, it proves you don't know Him, because to know Him is to love Him, and to love Him is to serve Him.'

Conquering Your Circumstances (4:10-20)

Verse 10 introduces one of the loveliest receipts ever written. Paul is rejoicing that their love and interest have found an opportunity to express themselves in the tangible form of a love-gift. Philip Henman, a Christian business-man, used to say, 'He who gives quickly, gives twice!' The Lord who linked Paul and the Philippian church had been the Inspirer of the gift ('In the Lord'), and this thought intensifies the joy he feels. His sense of joy and blessing are not suppressed nor extinguished between each gift he receives, for he is basically **content whatever the circumstances, verse 11.** In 1 Timothy 6:5 and 6, Paul contrasts the robbers who think that 'godliness is a means to financial gain' (verse 5), with his own view that 'godliness with contentment is great gain' (verse 6). He maintains a fine balance between his gratitude for their gift, and his spiritual freedom and independence. He is well able to defend his right to full pay for his preaching (1 Cor. 9:3-18; Gal. 6:6), but could preach free of charge as a means of answering his critics. His words to the Thessalonians back up this approach. 'You know we never used flattery, nor did we put on a mask to cover up greed... Surely you remember, brothers, our toil and hardship; we worked night and day in order not to be a burden to anyone while we preached the gospel of God to you' (1 Thess. 2:5, 9). His Christian life and his Christian joy are not sustained by 'shots in the arm' like monetary gifts.

In **verse 12** he reviews a life in Christian service in terms independent of circumstances. His swings of circumstances have not been matched by mood swings. He has been able to avoid being so dominated by need, or rendered so complacent by having plenty, that in both of these situations he has forgotten God. He has often been in situations of restriction and need (see Acts 14:19; 16:22-25; 17:13;

18:12; 20:3; 2 Cor. 4:11; 6:4-5; 11:27, 33). He had been a leading Pharisee, and even as a Christian he had known situations of 'plenty' (Acts 16:15, 40; 16:33-34; 20:33-34; 28:2; Phil. 4:15, 16, 18). The verb translated **to have plenty** has primary reference to well-fed livestock. It is often a bigger temptation to be in situations of plenty. We can get sloppy and waste God's money by copying the lifestyle of the anti-God system around us. He calls the answer to this problem of being contented a **secret** (from the perfect passive form of the verb *mueo* 'to initiate'), a term used in the mystery religions. In the development of the gospel, the secret is now an open secret, a curtain drawn back to disclose what was previously hidden.

The Christian gospel does not deal in two-tiered truth, with one level for an eager elite; rather the 'secrets' are unveiled to every believer. In the mystery religions, revelation is sequential after initiation. But here in **verse 13**, Paul lets everyone know his secret of contentment – the inner strengthening of Christ who makes him able to face anything. His life is a blend of victory and humility. He lives each day in the Lord's presence, with the Supporter (a good translation of *Parakletos*, the 'One-called-alongside'). He is not self-sufficient, but he is Christ-sufficient. Even in his weakness (2 Cor. 12:10), or in prison, the Lord stood by his side (2 Tim. 4:17), making him strong.

From **verse 14** the apostle takes up the theme of thanks from verse 10. Their giving indicated partnership in his troubles. The word **troubles** (*thlipsei*) is pressure or friction, like the chafing caused by metal restraints on a prisoner's limbs. Their staged support marked out their special relationship in the early days of missionary service (verse 15). *dosis* and *lempsis* are financial trading terms for **giving** (the Philippians) and **receiving** (Paul). Paul left Macedonia in a hurry, according to Acts 17:14, when he moved on from Thessalonica to Athens and Corinth (2 Cor. 11:8-9). The young Philippian church had already helped when he was in Thessalonica.

He moves the scale of their giving from the carping criticism of his opponents at a mundane level (2 Cor. 11:7; 12:14; 1 Thess. 1:3, 5, 8.), to the dimension of Christian giving as an expression of worship, like incense, as a 'fragrant offering' or an acceptable sacrifice' (see Gen. 4:4; 8:21; Exod. 29:18; Rom. 12:1; 2 Cor. 2:15-16). The use of incense in pagan religion was based on the idea that the fragrance offered reached the nostrils of a grateful deity. In 2 Corinthians 2:15 and 16, Paul draws on the festival atmosphere of the celebration of a general's triumph in the streets of Rome. The buildings would be garlanded with flowers, and the streets strewn with flower-petals. The air would be heavy with the mellifluous sounds and odours of burning incense offered in thanks to the Roman gods for victory granted. Paul writes 'for we are the aroma of Christ'. In other words, every church should be a fragrance factory!

CHRISTLIKENESS

Not only in the words you speak,
Not only by your deeds confessed,
But in the most unconscious way
Is Christ expressed.
Is it a beatific smile?
A holy light upon your brow?
Oh, no! I felt His presence when you laughed just now.
For me, 'twas not the truth you taught,
To you so clear, to me so dim,
But when you came yourself you
Brought a sense of Him.
And from your eyes He beckons me

And from your heart His love is shed,
Till I lose sight of you, and see
The Christ instead.

In **verse 18**, Paul again uses words frequently used in financial technical terms, like **I have received** (*apecho*) **full payment**.

In **verse 19**, Paul becomes touchingly personal – **my God** – and earmarks Him as the Supplier of our need. God's generosity does not mean that we should live wastefully. We cannot expect Him to cater for either greed or luxuries. When the famous violinist Fritz Kreisler was admitted to the Vienna Conservatory of Music, he was their youngest ever student, aged seven. In addition to his musical ability, he spoke eight languages, and was thoroughly competent in philosophy, history and mathematics. He was, of course, an outstanding violinist. He regarded his musical ability as God's gift, and called the money he earned 'public money', a resource entrusted to his care for proper distribution. Kreisler would not regard his view as normative for others. In spite of his world-wide success, he and his wife would never go out to a restaurant to buy a meal, nor would they buy a home. Kreisler said, with great feeling, that between him and a home of his own stood all the homeless people in the world. He never failed to thank God for all His kindness to him. The Philippians who had given to Paul would find with Christians across the generations that God's shovel is bigger than theirs! God's giving was not in proportion to theirs, but according to His glorious riches in Christ Jesus. The glory is that of the Shekinah, the shining presence of God in the Tabernacle, or Tent-shrine. 'Moses could not enter the Tent of Meeting because the cloud had settled on it, and the glory of the LORD filled the Tabernacle' (Exod. 40:35). There is a distinction between 'out of' and 'according to' God's glorious riches. This is no penny-pinching handout, but a generosity with style, appropriate to the God who owns the world's livestock and mineral wealth! (see Psalm 50:10-11; Haggai 2:8). There is no doubt about the inherent riches vested in Christ ('For you know the grace of our Lord Jesus Christ, that though He was rich, yet for your sakes He became poor, so that you through His poverty might become rich, 2 Cor. 8:9). Here the stress is on the generous heart of the Father giving 'according to', not 'out of' (*kata* rather then *ek*) the resources of the Son. These are the resources of salvation and grace and a smiling providence, covering material as well as spiritual resources. As on all the New Testament themes of giving, the glory that is His by right is reflected in the doxology of verse 20.

Final Farewells (4:21-23)

Verse 21 is all-embracing in greeting everyone at Philippi, and he includes his immediate companions in the work of the Lord, and all the believers at, most probably (see introduction), Rome. **The saints who belong to Caesar's household** (verse 22) probably refers to those in his service as government employees rather than the members of his family. The doxology in verse 23, with grace as the keynote (see comment on 1:1), complements the doxology of verse 21 with glory as its keynote. This grace reaches down into the human spirit, which responds to grace, and experiences grace.

QUESTIONS FOR DISCUSSION – 4:1-23

1. Please discuss the factors which are most likely to cause trouble in churches.

2. Read 4:2 with the teaching of our Lord in Matthew 18:15-17. Should a church have a policy on conflict management? Should we/could we take steps to prevent trouble-makers from moving round the churches?

3. How can we foster (a) increased rejoicing (b) increased prayer, individually and corporately?

4. Using verses 8-9, could you discuss the topic, 'A Christian's Thinking.'

5. Outline a talk you could give on the theme 'Christian Contentment'.

6. Could you summarise your church's policy and practices on giving? Is there any help for us on this subject in this passage of scripture (see for example verse 14 onwards)? Do you think new Christians/church members should be given teaching about giving?

PREACHING OUTLINES

OUTLINE 1

'IN CHRIST, AT PHILIPPI'
Philippians 1:1

INTRODUCTION: Salvation and Location go together at the heart of Paul's thinking. You have to act as a saved person where you are.

IN CHRIST

1. As our *Natural Environment*. The 'saints' are always plural! Translated, Born again, transformed.

2. As our *Family Relationship*. Just as in a natural family, we are loved for what we are, rather than what we achieve, and for what we are brought into....

3. As our *Dominating Influence*. Jesus, rather than Caesar or Satan, has won us, and controls us. 'Caesar is Lord' was the pagan fashion. 'Jesus is my Lord' is the normal Christian confession (see Romans 10:9).

AT PHILIPPI

Living for Jesus, here and now, the life of the Age to Come

In terms of Christian Strategy, God's Careful Plan. (Illustration: 'Vogue magazine is Read by the Overwhelming Minority of people.') Philippi a 'nucleating centre for the Gospel'.

In terms of Christian Ministry, God's Servant Role. Serve the Lord and Wash the Feet (see John 13:1ff.)

OUTLINE 2

INVOLVED IN A WORK OF GOD

Philippians 1:6: 'Being confident of this, that He who began a good work in you will carry it through to completion until the day of Christ Jesus.'

THE WORK HAS BEGUN! 1:6.

Three Criteria Met – Acts 16. The Lord's servants have seen, or been involved with:

Obedience to God's Call (Acts 16:6-10)

Operation of God's Spirit (Acts 16:14, 18, 26, 29-31)

Opposition to God's Church (Acts 16:19-24)

YOUR EARTHLY LOCATION

Servants ... at Philippi ...

YOUR HEAVENLY VOCATION

Saints ... in Christ Jesus

OUTLINE 3

GOD'S GOOD WORK

Philippians 1:6: 'Being confident of this, that He who began a good work in you, will carry it through to completion until the day of Christ Jesus.'

A Consistent Pattern

Everything good is God-Initiated, in Creation/Society/The Life of the Believer.

A Careful Persistence

God continues work which he begins, not like the foolish Tower-builder in Jesus' story in Luke 14:28-30 (Illustration – 'McCaig's Folly/Tower, in Oban).

(Eph. 2:8, 9. Titus 3:4, 5.)

A Confident Promise

Be sure! God will bring His work through to perfection and maturity (Rom. 2:16; 2 Peter 3:10-12).

Samuel Rutherford asked: 'Is God ploughing in your life? – be encouraged; He purposes fruit.'

God is the Pioneer/Pursuer/Perfecter of good work.

OUTLINE 4

OUR UTMOST FOR HIS HIGHEST

Philippians 1:9-11: 'And this is my prayer: that your love may abound more and more in knowledge and depth of insight, that you may be able to discern what is best and may be pure and blameless until the day of Christ, being filled with the fruits of righteousness that comes through Jesus Christ – to the glory and praise of God.'

PRESERVED – by a Common Life/A Constraining Love/ A Central Lord

  and

PRAYED FOR (vv. 4-9): Emphasise the importance of Prayer in any work of God.

Prayer as a confession of need, an exposure to God, an unselfish/life-changing encounter.

1. A MULTIPLIED LOVE: 9a
2. AN EXPANDED PERCEPTION: 9b
3. A HEIGHTENED DISCERNMENT: 10a
4. A PURIFIED CHARACTER: 10b
5. A ROUNDED PERSONALITY: 11a

What a Fellowship!
What a Prayer!
What a Lord!

OUTLINE 5

WHAT IS THE GOSPEL?

'Now I want you to know, brothers, that what has happened
to me has really served to advance the gospel.'

Paul moves from his Prayer as a Partner to his Position as
a Prisoner (Phil. 1:12. 1 Cor. 15:1ff).

Gospel an Important Theme – 1:5, 7, 12, 14. Word of
God 1:16, 27.

A SPIRIT-GIVEN STORY

Shared Truth (1 Cor. 15:1, 3) – passing on a Treasure.
Solid Truth (1 Cor. 15:2) – A Basis on which to Lean.
A Belief by which to Live.
Supreme Truth (1 Cor. 15:3) – 'Of First Importance.'

A SELF-GIVING SEQUENCE

Centred on a Person (1 Cor. 15:3b – His Coming/Dying/
Rising)
Focussed on an Action 'For Our Sins'
(Sin characterised by Alienation, Bondage, and Conflict)

A SAVING SPECTACLE

'Appeared' several times.
The Need for a Vision of Christ.

OUTLINE 6

'KEEP IT SIMPLE, KEEP IT REAL'

Philippians 1:21: 'For to me, to live is Christ,
and to die is gain.'

INTRODUCTION: People sometimes complain about the Bible being too obscure and difficult. The Bible is like a harbour at a seaside resort – there are shallows in which children can paddle, and depths that can drown a man. The Mission of Jesus is summarised in words of one syllable in Luke 19:10, and Paul's attitude to life and death is summarised here in words of one syllable.

1. Christian Life is Personal: 'For to **me**'

In the context, Paul had been speaking about other people, false brothers, etc. Here he concentrates on his own view. How does this relate to us? Scripture Union magazine title summed it up: *JAM* = 'Jesus And Me'. What is religion? Christianity is essentially a personal relationship with Jesus Christ.

2. Christian Life is Practical: 'to live' (the Greek text is actually a present infinitive with the definite article, 'the to live', meaning the continuous process of living. Man from Harlem, New York, to Bruce Kenrick: 'it's alright you guys talking about life, we've got to live it.' Living the Gospel is a viable option for today. No verb 'is' in text – 'for to me to live, namely Christ i.e. Paul's boundaries in life are defined by Christ, he is the Christ-intoxicated man.

3. Christian Life is Profitable: 'and to die is gain'. Again, there is a definite article, this time with an Aorist infinitive, i.e. it refers to the one-off act of dying. Tertullian 'watch us, how we live, watch us, how we die'. The blood of the martyrs is the seed of the church. We usually tell bereaved people we are sorry to hear of their sad **loss.** Death would be a gain for Paul in two ways – it would advance the witness of God's people, and he would be with Christ, which is far better (see v.23, and 3:20, 21).

OUTLINE 7

'LIVING WORTHY OF THE GOSPEL'

Philippians 1:27-30: 'Whatever happens, conduct yourselves in a manner worthy of the gospel ...'

INTRODUCTION:

1. The gospel covers the place I'm in, and the people I'm with. Acrostic for *GOSPEL* – 'God Our Saviour Proclaims Eternal Life.'

2. We must Stand – *Sola Gratia* – 'Grace alone', not Merit; *Sola Fides* – 'Faith Alone', not Works; *Sola Scriptura* – 'Scripture alone', not Tradition.

3. We must Stay (DV) – See 1:24-26.

Illustration: At children's meeting where children were asked to put up their hand if they wanted to go to heaven. 'Put your hand up Jeannie, we're not going just now.'

4. Since we are staying, Relationships are important. For example, the most difficult problem in overseas mission is the relationships between missionaries.

WE NEED A CHARACTER BASED ON DUTY, (1:27a).

'Whatever happens, conduct yourselves in a manner worthy of the Gospel'. Roman Catholic children used to have 'holy days of obligation'. We are 'under obligation' (see Romans 1:14: Greeks and Non-Greeks).

Praise God and illustrate lives of Christians with a sense of duty.

WE NEED A CONVICTION BASED ON UNITY (1:27b-28).

'Standing Firm' for the faith of the Gospel, like a Sumo wrestler standing his ground.

'Showing Faith' in the witness of the Gospel, like a phalanx of soldiers together.

'Spurning Fear' in the defence of the Gospel, 'contending' (v. 27) courageous (v. 28).

WE NEED A COURAGE BASED ON DEITY (1:29).

There is no 'small print' with the Gospel.

An Adversity to be Shouldered (verse 29). If you believe in Jesus, you are guaranteed a hard time from the Devil!

An Identity to be Shared (verse 30). The Lord Jesus is with you in it! – 'My yoke' (Matt. 11:29).

OUTLINE 8

'TRAINING OUR MINDS'
Philippians 2:1-4: 'Make my joy complete
by being like-minded.'

INTRODUCTION: To harmonise the kind of conduct which is worthy of the Gospel (1:27) we have to 'get our minds right'. A right attitude is important – for ourselves, as well as for those around us in fellowship.

Chapter 2 has a focus on verse 5: 'Your attitude should be the same as Christ Jesus.'

There are three kinds of mind pictured here, in verses 1-4:

1. THE SELFISH MIND. The unhelpful aspects here, 'selfish ambition and vain conceit' (verse 3) are like weeds in the garden. The former word means hatred or rivalry between opponents, expressed in hostility, antagonism or contention. Some people's family life is an on-going soap-opera of strife, where people increase and lug along the baggage of the past. It is expressed in bad-mouthing, point-scoring and imposing your will on others. We become like hedgehogs, prickly and unapproachable. Sin should be repented of, confessed and forsaken.

The 'vain conceit' is expressed in Capital 'I' stories, and life-style – cars, hairdos, clothes, etc.

The selfish mind-set can be characterised by three words – acquisition, advantage, and advancement.

2. THE SINGLE MIND. Verse 2: 'Being likeminded, having the same love, being one in spirit and purpose.' Its features are:

(c) Christ-centred Encouragement (verse 1) since we have been forgiven and 'familied'. Illustrate.

(d) Love-based Comfort, arising out of His strengthening love for us.

(e) Spirit-focussed Fellowship (2 Cor. 13:14). A laminated phrase: 'Fellowship deriving from/resulting from the Spirit.'

(f) Sympathetic Concern. Going out to others in loving interest.

3. THE SUBMISSIVE MIND. Verse 3b: 'In humility consider others better than yourselves.' We need to develop the humility or modesty described in verse 3. In theological terms, humility is not a grace but a duty. It is not included in the Fruit of the Spirit in Galatians 5:22ff. It is an appropriate response to our position before God, which reflects in our relationship with others.

APPLICATION: We have to give up the Selfish Mind and crucify it.

We have to adopt the Single Mind and cultivate it.

We have to imitate the Submissive Mind and model it.

OUTLINE 9

'THE INNER NATURE OF JESUS'
Philippians 2:6: 'Who being in very nature God, did not consider equality with God something to be grasped'....

INTRODUCTION: Verses 1-4 deal with the Christian 'Mind-set'.

THE GLORY OF CHRIST'S PERSON
(John 17:5; John 1:1-2; Col. 1:15-17; Heb. 1:3.)
The Glory of a Mutual Affection (a Trinity of Love)
The Glory of a Sinless Perfection
The Glory of an Exact Representation (Image and Coinage)
The Glory of an Angelic Adoration
The Glory of a Creative Production

THE GLORY OF CHRIST'S PITY
Equality with God was neither:
A Plunder to be Grabbed
A Prize to be Grasped
Jesus was not like Lucifer or Adam
True Majesty: 'Down From His Glory'

THE GREATNESS OF OUR PRIVILEGES
He gives us Power to Believe in Him
He gives us Power to Belong to Him

OUTLINE 10

'JESUS THE SERVANT OF GOD'

Philippians 2:7: 'But made Himself nothing, taking the very nature of a servant.'

1. THE TRACES OF THE SERVANT

(a) In the Lives of the Old Testament Saints

Abraham (Ps. 105:42); Caleb (Num. 14:24)

Joshua (Josh. 24:29); David (2 Samuel 7:5-8 [twice])

Moses (12 times, classic passage Num. 12:7)

(b) In the Description of the Nation of Israel

(Is. 41:8-10; 44:21; 48:20; 49:3)

Towards a definition of Servant – someone who is at the disposal of someone else.

2. THE TRIALS OF THE SERVANT

Four Servant Songs (Is. 42:1-4; 49:1-6; 50:4-9; 52:13 – 53:12)

CHOSEN, MEEK, PATIENT, DISFIGURED, A PUBLIC SPECTACLE.

3. THE TRIUMPHS OF THE SERVANT

(Acts 3:13, 26; Acts 4:27, 30)

Nearest translation is 'boy' with overtones of servitude and inferiority.

John 13 and Hebrews 4: The Servant is Son.

A Servant King should have a Servant Church – Illustrate: We should be at His disposal to serve Him and worship Him in deeds as well as words.

OUTLINE 11

'EVEN DEATH ON A CROSS'

Philippians 2:8: 'And being found in appearance as a man, he humbled himself and became obedient to death – even death on a cross!'

INTRODUCTION: Illustrate: 'Going to great lengths for people.'

How far (down) did Christ go for us?

THE VILENESS OF THE CROSS

Its Shadowy Origins. Originated with Assyrians, famous for cruelty.

Its Shameful Associations. It was the lowest rung on the ladder of Christ's degradation. Routine execution of slaves (no rights or dignity).

Public humiliation – naked and nailed/tied. Ugly spikes, square in section.

Preliminary beating. Flogged/Mockery/Blood loss/ dehydration/flies.

Weight of the body fixed the thoracic cage so that lungs could not expel the inhaled air. Slow choking induced panic.

THE VALUE OF THE CROSS

It Made a Jewish Priest Redundant

It Made a Roman Pagan Respectful

It Made Christian Preachers Resourceful

It Makes Christian People Responsive

OUTLINE 12

'SALVATION WORK-OUT'

Philippians 2:12-18: 'Continue to work out your salvation with fear and trembling, for it is God who works in you....'

INTRODUCTION

From Downs and Ups to Ins and Outs. The way up for the Lord Jesus was the way down, (v. 6-11). Here we are to 'work out' (verse 12) as God 'works in' (verse 13).

Wherefore the Therefore? (Verse 12): Since:

1. Jesus the Son by His Self-emptying, Self-denying love has revealed His mind-set.

2. God the Father's stamp of approval confirms this mind-set.

3. The Holy Spirit of Jesus can give us strength to live according to this mind-set.

Then:

GET TO THE GYM! Work out what's worked in/work to a finish what God has begun (1:6).

1. A PURPOSE TO ACHIEVE (Verse 12)

Personal/Humble (verse 12)

Contented/Consecrated (verse 15)

2. A POWER TO RECEIVE (Verse 13)

God worked in: Moses (40 years); Jesus (the 18 hidden years).

Illustration: Roland Bell, OMF, a senior missionary who did his best work in his final years.

Are we motivated by outside pressure or inner power? (John 14:16-17; Acts 1:8; Bible /Prayer/ Hardship.)

3. A PROMISE TO BELIEVE (Verses 16-18)

Shining for Jesus ....

Running for Jesus ....

Rejoicing in Jesus ....

OUTLINE 13

COPYBOOK HUMILITY – TIMOTHY AND EPAPHRODITUS
Philippians 2:19ff

INTRODUCTION. Spurgeon said: 'We need sermons in boots rather than sermons in books.' Timothy and Epaphroditus embody the Jesus Mind-Set of the previous verses. Timothy was:

A Young Man (1 Tim. 4:12; 2 Tim. 2:1). Paul called him 'my son'.)
A Delicate Man (1 Tim. 5:23)
A Timid Man (2 Tim. 1:7; 2:2)

Yet the Lord did a wonderful work in his life. Greatly loved. Shaped by Parental Influence, Spiritual Gift, Christian Friendship, Divine Grace (see 2 Timothy 1:5-9). Timothy had:

A SERVANT'S HEAD. Not occupied by worldly concerns, but preoccupied with Christ.

A SERVANT'S HEART. Not loafing in the Master's 'absence', like a lazy servant, but labouring in His harvest field.

A SERVANT'S HOPE. Not uselessly shadow-boxing, but effectively profitable in the Lord's service.

OUTLINE 14

EPAPHRODITUS AND PAUL
Philippians 2:25-30

A 'Wounded healer' is the best kind to have alongside –
he's been through it before you have, and his sympathy
seems authentic.

He was characterised by:

Family Love

Fruitful Labour

Fighting Loyalty

EPAPHRODITUS AND THE PHILIPPIANS

Their Messenger

Their Minister

OUTLINE 15

'BACK TO THE BIG PICTURE'
Philippians 3:1: 'Finally, my brothers,
rejoice in the Lord!'

INTRODUCTION: 'Finally' cannot introduce after-thoughts, for there are 44 more verses! (see 1 Thessalonians 4:1 where there are 46 more verses). It has to be a summary phrase, like 'Well, then'... Here he resumes the 'Big Picture' of Joy.

He had written of circumstances likely to rob them of joy:

Imprisonment: 'Don't worry about me – to die is gain.'

False colleagues with wrong motives: Rejoice that Christ is being preached.

Jealousy/envy/division: Maintain your joy by retaining the 'Jesus Mind-set'.

Separation: God is at work in you wherever I am (2:13).

Illness: I am sending the brother who was ill back to you.

THE BIG PICTURE IS TO REJOICE! Like a repeated theme in overture or symphony –

It is a command, with resources within our scope to obey it.

It is not merely our emotions whipped up by a spiritual 'cheer leader'.

It is not artificially promoted by 'atmosphere', drink, drugs, or 'feel good factor'.

THE SOURCES OF OUR JOY

1. Our State, Our position in Christ (Eph. 1:3; John 16:33).

2. Our Circumstances. We have troubles, but we treat them as joy-promoters.

3. Our Saviour. Our testimony proclaims Him (1 Peter 2:9).

4. Ourselves. Nehemiah 8:10: 'The joy of the Lord is your strength.'

THE SAFEGUARDS OF OUR JOY

1. A Loose Hold on Human Reputation. As stewards of God's gifts, even if we lose the lot, we have lost nothing.

2. A Loose Hold on Human Heroes. Many of our Idols turn out to have feet of clay! (Illustrate: Jimmy Greaves, John Denver). Paul was maybe too important to the Philippians.

3. A Loose Hold on Human Props. Hebrews 13:5: 'I will never leave you nor forsake you.' 'Here is something that can never be touched, and is beyond the efforts of man to destroy' (Dr Martyn Lloyd Jones).

We can Rejoice as we: Monitor His Gifts, Medidate on His Person and Marvel at His Salvation.

OUTLINE 16

'WORSHIP – THE GENUINE ARTICLE'

Philippians 3:3: 'For it is we who are the circumcision, we who worship by the Spirit of God, who glory in Christ Jesus, and put no confidence in the flesh.'

INTRODUCTION: The letter is like a symphony, with repeated themes of peace and rejoicing. Sermon based on verse 3 here, 'worshipping by the spirit of God'.

DUPLICATION. Repetition has a valid place in our Christian lives, and is a constant component of good teaching. It is good to learn new things every day, but we need to reflect constantly on the 'old things' we first learned as Christians. Christian learning, like maths, is a sequential subject. Therefore it is not a chore for Paul to be repetitive, and it is a safeguard for the Philippian believers (see verse 1b).

DIRECTION. Watch out! (verse 2). Jesus gave this warning in Mark 13:33, so we have always to be on guard. Christians should always be wide awake to possible dilution of the Gospel and infiltration of the church. We should also be aware of the world around us. John Sung, after his intensive study courses, settled for the Bible and the newspaper for his daily reading.

DENUNCIATION. Paul uses 'topsy-turvy teaching' here, because Jews often referred to Gentiles as 'dogs', yet Paul uses the term here of Judaisers. He is thinking, not of pet dogs or lapdogs as the playthings of the rich, but of the pariah dogs, the mangy scavengers of the back-streets, who are unpredictable in their actions, indiscriminate in their tastes, and dangerous for everyone they bite and scratch. He then highlights the evil-doers, whose character is measured, not by what they say, but by how they behave. He reverts to 'topsy-turvy teaching' regarding circumcision, claiming that Christians, not Jews are the genuine article. True Circumcision is inward and spiritual (see Jeremiah 4:4. Romans 2:28).

DEFINITION. The apostle highlights three features of genuine worship here in verse 3:

1. It is Spirit-filled worship;
2. It is Christ-centred worship and
3. It is God-honouring worship 'no confidence in the flesh'.

We are made and saved and energised by a gracious God.

OUTLINE 17

'COUNTING PROFITS AND LOSSES'

Philippians 3:4-8: 'But whatever was to my profit, I counted loss for the sake of Christ.'

INTRODUCTION: Rejoicing, Watchful and Authentic, (verses 1-3).

PERSONAL CONTRAST: Paul and the Judaisers (verse 4).

PARENTAL CONTRIBUTIONS: Advantages listed in (verse 5).

Ecclesiastical: 'Circumcised on the eighth day.' Not a proselyte.

National: 'Of the people of Israel.'

Ancestral: Of the Tribe of Benjamin, the favourite.

Family: 'A Hebrew of the Hebrews' (Hebrew-speaking son of Hebrew parents).

PAST CONQUESTS (verses 5 and 6)

A Separatist : 'In regard to the Law, a Pharisee' (Jewish Scripture Union group).

An Enthusiast: 'As for zeal, persecuting the church.'

A Purist: 'As for legal righteousness, faultless.'

PRESENT CONSIDERATIONS

Calculation and Consecration. 'Who switched the Price Tags?' Revised Values, Revered Lord.

OUTLINE 18

'THE BEST KIND OF KNOWLEDGE – KNOWING JESUS'

Philippians 3:10-11: 'I want to know Christ, and the power of his resurrection, and the fellowship of sharing in his sufferings, becoming like him in his death, and so, somehow, to attain to the resurrection from the dead.'

INTRODUCTION: Phrases of desire and determination in purpose clauses like verse 8, 'that I may gain Christ' and verse 9, 'and be found in Him'. The form of the verb in verse 10 has inherent purpose – we have to supply 'I want' to join 'to know Him'. Paul wants to know:

1. THE PERSON OF HIS LORD: 'I want to know Christ'. Spiritually and personally rather than cerebrally, not studying a book, but being absorbed by a Person. Communication leads to observation, and captivation.

2. THE POWER OF HIS LIFE: 'And the power of His resurrection', may be the power that is His resurrection, or the power emanating from His resurrection. The dunamis of Jesus is a life-changing experience.

3. THE PASSION OF HIS LOVE: 'and the fellowship of sharing in His suffering.' God's love is 'holy love' as P. T. Forsyth said, but it is also suffering love. Never able to enter fully into His sufferings, but many Christians have shared in His suffering to some extent. (Illustrate: Richard Wurmbrandt, who suffered for about thirteen years in

189

Romanian Communist prisons, and has permanent scars on his body).

4. THE PARTNERSHIP OF HIS LOSS: 'becoming like Him in His death.' This means, literally, 'sharing the shape' of His death, conforming to a personal crucifixion (see Galatians 2:20). Persecution and martyrdom. (Verse 11 does not specify the route, but His power in action will do the needful (see also 1 Corinthians 15:22 and 52).

'To Know Him is to Love Him. To Love Him is to Obey Him. To Obey Him is to Serve Him.'

OUTLINE 19
(CHILDREN'S TALK)

'PRESSING ON TO WIN THE PRIZE'

Philippians 3:12-14: 'Forgetting what is behind, and straining toward what is ahead, I press on toward the goal to win the prize....'

ONE TEAM FOR THE CUP

A FEW ATHLETES FOR MEDALS

Mark 8:36

ANYONE FOR ETERNAL LIFE

God's offer is as wide as our sin is deep. Sin the only hurdle to peace with God.

OUTLINE 20

'SINGLE-MINDED SERVICE'
Philippians 3:13-14: 'But one thing I do.'

INTRODUCTION: Opportunity for reflection in jail, for Paul. 'Grow old gracefully, having done my little bit?' Not at all! Read Text (no verb 'to be' in the original).

THE CHRISTIAN PLEASES ONE MASTER
New Testament is clear on the folly of trying to serve two masters: Matthew 6:24; James 1:3: 'A double-minded man is unstable in all his ways.' Romans 6:16 on slavery. Second Timothy 2:4: 'no soldier on active service gets involved in civilian pursuits.' 2 Corinthians 5:9: 'We make it our aim ... to please Him.' Paul was not man's, but God's servant. He was not under Caesar, but under Christ. Apply to work situations, and pleasing employers.

THE CHRISTIAN PURSUES ONE ACTIVITY
Christian life is action rather than contemplation, although there is a place for thought and meditation. There is a balance between devotion and duty. But there is one focus, one governing principle – serving God as a citizen of heaven, 3:20. Why dissipate our energies? 'One thing I do'. True of our community life as a church as well as our individual lives. Easy to be side-tracked into secondary or negative activities.

THE CHRISTIAN PREPARES FOR ONE REWARD

'The athletic metaphor' – straining for the tape and the prize. Christians have a target – aim at nothing and you will be sure to hit it! Paul always had reward as a spur behind him and a goal before him. Some Christians think it is unworthy, but Jesus had reward in His teaching – the Talents and Pounds parables. Christ is the Prize, verses **8, 10**, 1:23; 1 Timothy 4:7, **8**; 2 Timothy 4:7, **8**. We should not be squandering God's gifts, but harnessing every ounce of energy into doing His will. Illustration from chief's son in Brazilian tribe, when Robert Kennedy asked him what he liked doing best – 'I like best being occupied with Jesus' (story from Des Derbyshire of Wycliffe Bible Translators).

OUTLINE 21

'THREE KEY QUESTIONS'

Philippians 3:20-21: 'But our citizenship is in heaven. And we eagerly await a Saviour from there, the Lord Jesus Christ.'

INTRODUCTION: The thread of Christian living is given in verses 1-2, namely, rejoicing and watching, and the threat to Christian living is given in verses 18-19. The worst thing a church can do is to appoint unspiritual men to spiritual office (see 1 Timothy 3).

Our text exposes three key questions about Christian living:

1. WHERE DO YOU BELONG? 'But our citizenship is in heaven' (verse 20). The Romans adapted Alexander the Great's ideas about settling colonies of veterans and wounded soldiers in conquered areas to secure them for the occupying power. Philippi was a Roman colony, like a piece of Italy transplanted there. People born there were treated as if they were born in Rome. The Christian's homeland is in heaven:

We have **heavenly loyalties** (4:3) Our names are written in the Book of Life (Rev. 20:12ff). In Luke 10:20 Jesus gives this high priority, and the text uses a Greek perfect tense i.e. they were written and this has continuing effects.

We speak **heavenly language**. Our speech reveals our inner motivation (Matt. 12:34-37; Eph. 4:29). Our speech is not earth-bound to the world's iniquity, arrogance, pollution, corrosion and corruption.

'There is no sounder test of whether people are truly Christians or not, than their view of life in this world' (Dr M. Lloyd-Jones). Colossians 3:2: 'Set your minds on things above.'

We obey heaven's laws. We are givers, not getters. Jesus thought of others before Himself (2 Cor. 5:14, 15). The evidence of selfishness is in flesh-energised self-glory.

2. WHAT DO YOU EXPECT?

Not, surely, big houses, cars, bank balances etc. Surrounded by our enemies and haunted by our weaknesses we need Someone/Something to look forward to. Jesus is the Conqueror of the forces of darkness, a coming Saviour rather than a vengeful Judge. We look for Him (Acts 1:11).

3. HOW ARE THINGS GOING TO CHANGE?

There will be an end of groaning (Rom. 8:22-23). An end of Fallen-ness, weakness, corruptibility, and mortality, and a changed 'me'. Renovated. Refashioned. Refurbished. Reprogrammed. Involves the spirit, soul and body (1 Thess. 5:23). Christ's unleashed energy ('energia' rather than 'dunamis') and sovereign mastery are able to do all this.

OUTLINE 22

A NEW YEAR MESSAGE
Philippians 4:6-9.
Three Secrets for a Happy New Year.

Read especially 4:6-7: 'Do not be anxious about anything, but in everything, by prayer and petition, with thanksgiving, present your requests to God. And the peace of God, which transcends all understanding, will guard your hearts and minds in Christ Jesus.'

GODLY PRAYER – Prayer ... Petition ... Thanksgiving ... cover every situation at home or at work. Loneliness/Worry/ Fear.

Prayer sets things in perspective, and puts our wills in line with the will of God.

Prayer releases the resources to win and to cope.

GODLY PEACE

The Peace of God comes from the God of Peace (verse 9).

The Peace which Christ gives is a positive gift rather than a pious greeting.

GODLY PROTECTION

THE GARRISON TOWN: Philippi was a garrison town. Soldiers always in evidence.

THE GUARDED HEART: Soldiers always on guard, even through the night. A very positive image of Peace as 'Peace the Warrior'....

OUTLINE 23

'GOD'S AMAZING GENEROSITY'

Philippians 4:19: 'And my God will meet all your needs according to his glorious riches in Christ Jesus.'

INTRODUCTION: Paul was not in the ministry for the money! He writes in 1 Thessalonians 2:5: 'You know we never used flattery, nor did we put on a mask to cover up greed – God is our witness.' He was a tent-maker, and continued to practise his skill of tent-making (Acts 18:3). Verses 11-13 here in Philippians 4 make that plain also. He deals with giving and receiving in verse 15, and tries hard to maintain the balance between the Philippians' kindness, and his independence. Remember Abraham and the King of Sodom (Gen. 14:23: 'I will accept nothing belonging to you, not even a thread, or the thong of a sandal, so that you will never be able to say, "I made Abram rich"'). Paul sets out three great principles of Christian liberality here:

Generosity is a Character Test. Our love is expressed in what/how we give (Luke 7:44-47).

Generosity is a Spiritual Investment (verse 17). See the surprising teaching in Luke 16:9.

The writer once pointed out to a farmer who kindly allowed a Scripture Union canvas camp for 75 boys to be held in his field 'This is not an investment in turnips!'

Generosity is a Worshipful Act (verse 18). The sweet smell of sacrificial giving is like the aroma of a rose on a fresh spring morning. Proverbs 19:17 links giving to the poor and the Lord Himself: 'He who is kind to the poor lends to the Lord'

197

Philippians 4:19 indicates :

A Gracious Saviour I can Trust. 'My God' ... Paul had proved God for many years, and in every situation.

A Great Supply I can Trace. 'Your need' ... God will supply all our need, not our greed or our luxuries.

A Golden Security I can Tap. 'His Riches'... Contrast with the Reserves which banks state they have, God's reserves and resources are unlimited, safeguarded in Christ, and shared with His people. Not a penny-pinching handout, but given 'according to', with style and panache appropriate to His divine character.

BOOKS CONSULTED

B. and K. Aland, M. Black, C. Martins, B.M. Metzger, and A. Wikgren, editors. *The Greek New Testament*, Fourth revised Edition. United Bible Societies. 1993.

W. Bauer, *A Greek-English Lexicon*, Second Edition revised and augmented by F.W. Gingrich and F.W. Danker from W. Bauer's Fifth edition. University of Chicago Press. 1979.

S. Briscoe, *Bound for Joy*. Regal Books, 1975.

F.F. Bruce, *Philippians*, The New International Bible Commentary, Paternoster Press, 1989.

F.F. Bruce, Paul, *Apostle of the Free Spirit*, Paternoster Press, Revised edition 1980.

I. Coffey, *Philippians, Free to be God's People*, Crossway Books, 1994.

G.B. Duncan, *Preach the Word*, Marshall Pickering, 1989.

M.J. Erickson, *Christian Theology*, Baker Book House, 1991.

J. Fergusson, *An Exposition of the Epistles of Paul*, Sovereign Grace Publishers, Evansville, Indiana.

D. Guthrie, *New Testament Introduction*, The Pauline Epistles, Tyndale Press, 1961.

G.F. Hawthorne, *Philippians*, Word Bible Commentary, Word Publishing, Milton Keynes, 1991.

W. Hendriksen, *A Commentary on the Epistle to the Philippians*, A Geneva Series Commentary, Banner of Truth Trust, 1963.

A.M. Hunter, *Galatians to Colossians*, Layman's Bible Commentaries, SCM Press, 1960.

H.R. Jones, *Philippians*, Focus on the Bible, Christian Focus Publications, 1993.

J.B. Lightfoot, *Philippians*, Crossway Classic Commentaries, Crossway Books, 1994.

D.M. Lloyd-Jones, *The Life of Joy*, and *The Life of Peace* (2 volumes), Hodder and Stoughton, 1993.

J. V. McGee, *Through the Bible Commentaries*, Thomas Nelson, 1991.

I.H. Marshall, *Philippians*, Epworth Press, 1991.

R.P. Martin, *Philippians*, Tyndale New Testament Commentaries. Revised edition. Inter Varsity Press, 1994.

R.P. Martin, Articles 'Philippi' and 'Philippians' in *Illustrated Bible Dictionary*, Part 3. IVP, reprinted 1988.

E.K. Milliken, *The Roman People*, G.G. Harrap and Co, London, 1951.

J.A. Motyer, *The Richness of Christ*, Studies in the Letter to the Philippians. Inter Varsity Fellowship, 1966.

J.A. Motyer, *The Message of Philippians*, Bible Speaks Today series, Inter-Varsity Press, 1984.

P. T. O'Brien, *The Epistle to the Philippians*, A Commentary on the Greek Text. Eerdmans, Grand Rapid, Michgan 1991.

A.T. Robertson, *Paul's Joy in Christ* and *Paul and the Intellectuals*, Broadman Press, 1917.

The Ryrie Study Bible, New American Standard translation, Moody Press, 1976.

J. Shields, *Philippian Studies and Bible Readings*, Hulbert Publishing Company.

H.D.M. Spence and J.S. Exell, editors, *Ephesians, Philippians, Colossians*, The Pulpit Commentary, Funk and Wagnalls Co, London, 1911.

N. Turner, *Christian Words*, T. and T. Clark, Edinburgh, 1980.

M.R. Vincent, *Philippians and Philemon*, International Critical Commentary, T. and T. Clark, Edinburgh, 1902.

W.E. Vine, *Expository Dictionary of New Testament Words*, Oliphants, 1970.

W.W. Wiersbe, *Be Joyful*, Chariot Victor Publishing, SP Publications, 1974.